INDIFFERENCE TO DIFFERENCE

INDIFFERENCE TO DIFFERENCE

On Queer Universalism

MADHAVI MENON

UNIVERSITY OF MINNESOTA PRESS
MINNEAPOLIS · LONDON

Portions of chapter 2 were previously published as "Desire," in *Early Modern Theatricality*, ed. Henry S. Turner, 327–45 (Oxford: Oxford University Press, 2013); reprinted by permission of Oxford University Press. Portions of chapter 2 were previously published as "Of Cause," in "Shakespeare and Theory," ed. Francois Xavier Gleyzon and Johann Gregory, special issue, *English Studies* 94, no. 3 (May 2013): 278–90. A version of the Coda appeared as "Partition and Universalism: A Queer Theory," in "Queer Theory without Antinormativity," ed. Elizabeth Wilson and Robyn Wiegman, special issue, *differences* 26, no. 1 (May 2015): 117–40.

Published by the University of Minnesota Press
111 Third Avenue South, Suite 290
Minneapolis, MN 55401-2520
http://www.upress.umn.edu

Library of Congress Cataloging-in-Publication Data
Menon, Madhavi.
    Indifference to difference : on queer universalism / Madhavi Menon.
    Includes bibliographical references and index.
    ISBN 978-0-8166-9590-4 (hc)
    ISBN 978-0-8166-9592-8 (pb)
    1. Individualism in literature. 2. Individualism in art. 3. Equality in literature.
4. Social comparison. 5. Identity politics. I. Title.
    PN56.I57M46 2015
    809´.93353—dc23   2014043039

Printed in the United States of America on acid-free paper

The University of Minnesota is an equal-opportunity educator and employer.

21 20 19 18 17 16 15   10 9 8 7 6 5 4 3 2 1

For Gil

Kaun maqsad ko ishq bina pahuncha
Aarzu ishq muddaa hai ishq

Contents

Acknowledgments

This is my Delhi book. Not only was much of it written in the city, but also all of it was inspired by the syncreticism that is at the heart of Delhi. Indifference is here an unremarkable way of life.

Judith Brown, Kathryn Schwarz, an anonymous reader for the Press, and Richard Morrison, all read the manuscript and gave me suggestions in keeping with the high levels of their brilliance. Also at the University of Minnesota Press: Danielle M. Kasprzsak and Erin Warholm-Wohlenhaus. Special thanks to Cherene Holland for being the loveliest copyeditor in the universe.

Mahmood Farooqui and Danish Husain introduced me to the dazzling world of *dastangoi*; without them I would never have met Chouboli. Several kind friends, patient colleagues, and good interlocutors—you know who you are—went through the process of thinking and writing with me, and to you all I am immensely grateful.

Thanks and love to four sets of people: my parents for suffering me gladly; Nikhil and Rohan in the Land of the Bumbley Boo; Lee Edelman, whose warmth is sheltering; and Gil Harris, to whose color-filled being I can never be indifferent.

Introduction

Indifference

Some years ago, an immigration officer noticed that I had written "Professor" as my occupation on the visitor's form. He asked me what I taught. When I said "English literature," his eyes lit up—it turned out that he had studied English at university. He then asked if I specialized in authors like V. S. Naipaul and Salman Rushdie. I smiled and said no, I work on Shakespeare. His smile faded a little and was replaced by an expression of surprise. "Shakespeare," the unspoken comment asked? But, and a quick glance down at my passport confirmed this, wasn't I Indian . . . ?

Such surprise, which I often encounter, is born not of the malevolence of my particular interlocutor, but from a belief that identity should be immediately and physically recognizable. It is frequently assumed that English professors from India will teach Indian authors and that Indians will study them. To align matters even more closely, I'd been asked if I worked on Indian authors who'd traveled out of India, just like I had. My immigration officer wanted to know about traveling Indians from a traveling Indian—he wanted an authentic picture of difference undistorted by the colonizing gaze of those who are not, for instance, traveling Indians. Despite being motivated by a desire for difference, then, this thirst for knowledge detailed in advance the parameters within which that difference could be known and disseminated—Indians will study and teach Indian writers.

This book attempts to rethink the line of predictability that gets drawn from the body to identity, and from desire to the self. It is intended, in Julian Murphet's words, as a "labour of intellectual negation" (154) that asks us to undo certain protocols of ontological knowing.[1] As against the investment in difference that marks our current iterations of identity politics,

1

such labor necessitates taking seriously the politics of *indifference*. Invested as it is with all the explosiveness of a signifier that lives in difference, indifference argues for a radical break with the identity that undergirds liberal and conservative politics alike.

But first, let us step back a little. Used for many years as the platform from which to launch human rights movements of various stripes, identity politics and the multiculturalism it spawned has been extremely useful politically. As David Theo Goldberg defines it, "Broadly conceived, multiculturalism is critical of and resistant to the necessarily reductive imperatives of monocultural assimilation" (7).[2] But in the spectrum of multicultural resistance, the dominant strain has been and is now again what Terence Turner terms "difference multiculturalism" (413), in which homage paid to difference engenders conformity rather than revolution.[3] What starts out as an acknowledgment of difference devolves into a mandating of it. And as soon as politics starts making difference the basis of particular truths, we run into the problem of ontology that undergirds "difference multiculturalism."[4]

In their defense of identity politics, Satya P. Mohanty and Linda Martín Alcoff state that, in itself, "identity politics is neither positive nor negative. At its minimum, it is a claim that identities are politically relevant, an irrefutable fact. Identities are the locus and nodal point by which political structures are played out, mobilized, reinforced, and sometimes challenged. . . . Obviously, identities can be recognized in pernicious ways . . . [b]ut it is a false dilemma to suppose that we should *either* accept pernicious uses of identity or pretend they do not exist" (7).[5] It is absolutely correct that, in itself, nothing is positive or negative; Hamlet famously said the same thing several hundred years ago: "There is nothing either good or bad but thinking makes it so" (2.2.244–5).[6] However, as Michel Foucault has already pointed out in his analyses of power, to talk about identity as a *cause* by which people get classified is to put the cart before the horse.[7] For Foucault, even as identity has many real and often nasty effects, *it is also itself an effect*. Identity is the demand made by power—tell us who you are so we can tell you what you can do. And by complying with that demand, by parsing endlessly the particulars that make our identity different from one another's, we are slotting into a power structure, not dismantling it. We should never have to choose *between* good and bad identity, difference and universalism, but rather, our interrogation should focus on what subtends the demand for identity and difference. Critiquing identity politics, then, is not a dismissal of lived reality but, rather, a response to the oppressive demands that identity itself can make under the guise of a progressive politics. Oppression by identity also qualifies as lived experience, and we should not settle on a demand made by power without also taking seriously the consequences of that demand.

If anything, the most widespread truth about our lived reality is that it is too multiple to abide by a code of identitarian difference: *lived reality is at odds with identity politics.* This is why it is so startling when many of us seem content with thinking of our lives strictly within the structures that constrain it, speaking unironically about the immutability of race or gender or sexuality. Race and sex and gender and class are certainly policed fiercely in all societies, but why do we confuse that policing with the truth about ourselves? If anything, the categorization is the problem, not our challenging of it. In a bizarre move of sympathizing with our oppressors, we take to heart regimes that restrict us, and then tell ourselves that the restriction is the truth of our being in the world.

Indeed, any sense of acknowledging the superabundance of identity is fiercely policed by national and international law. Take, for instance, the case of Caster Semenye, the South African "hermaphroditic" athlete, who had to undergo testing to prove she was not "really" a man. Or various eugenics projects that measure genetic percentages to determine the minimum level of difference that can serve as an identity. In a more recent case, an Indian athlete was stripped of her medals on the presumption that she had a penis. Pinki Pramanik was arrested on a charge of rape; she was put in a men's ward in prison despite identifying and living as a woman, and treated with horror by the police and the media. Even after extensive tests conducted by a team of gynecologists, radiologists, and other specialists, however, Pramanik's sex was hard to determine.[8] There is perhaps nothing like sex to bring us face-to-face with the failure of regimes of identity. There is also nothing like sex to make us violently insist on identity nonetheless.

But it is not just sex—all manner of desire and fantasy is policed lest it lead to an acknowledgment of shifting identities. Think of Frantz Fanon's Antillean boy in *Black Skin, White Masks,* who identifies with the white oppressors in comic books and does not recognize himself in and as the Negro who is oppressed. The Antillean projects himself into the image of the hero-adventurer and disregards (or does not register) any somatic similarities the comic book might try and portray between himself and the outwitted and oppressed Negro. According to Fanon, it is only after the

Antillean boy goes to France that his fantasy life is discounted and negritude is made to stick to him as his identity.[9] Soma and psyche are grafted onto one another and the black boy is expected to behave not like the hero but like the underdog. Whether this graft is malevolent or supportive, it effects a unity of being that completely discounts desire and fantasy. By investing in somatic difference as the *truth* of one's particularity, identity politics counterintuitively reifies the frame of oppression it claims to be undermining. Such a craze for identity flies in the face of how we actually live and underestimates the surprising ways in which desire works all around us, every day. People are not one-difference ponies—we usually have many horses in the race. Every instance of flouted identity reminds us of that.

Indeed, this view of identity-as-constraint is precisely what Goldberg goes on to note:

> It has been pointed out commonly that identity can be exclusionary of those who are outside its scope; those who are—or who are taken to be— in no way affiliated. You don't belong, you don't meet the conditions or criteria of belonging so we are going to keep you out. What is less observed is that identity can also be a bondage within. It can keep people in who don't want to be in. And it can do so by insisting on an essential racial character, or simply by requiring racial solidarity. (12)

In an intellectual, social, and political milieu that prides itself on celebrating difference, ethnicities, religions, and sexualities are considered to be important because they are different from one another rather than deemed to be important for *being* different from one another. Different literatures are valued for what they can tell us about particular cultures. The value placed on difference acquires a premium when it is embodied by a person who is him- or herself different. Thus, Indian literature taught by an actual Indian is deemed to be better than Indian literature taught by a Chinese professor, an insistence that fundamentally discounts the imaginative leap literature insists we take. Slavoj Žižek notes that his "main criticism of identity politics is not its 'particularism' *per se* but, rather, its partisans' ubiquitous insistence that one's particular position of enunciation legitimizes or even guarantees the authenticity of one's speech" (328).[10] While difference is valued for its apparent ability to cross borders, it is even more prized when those borders are closed against the threat of inauthentic strangers. In practice, the value placed on difference is negated by the fixity with which embodiments of difference are policed.

How might we resist such a universal regime of difference that fixes difference into identity? How might we institute a project of antiphilosophy that opposes the certainty of identitarian knowledge? For Alain Badiou, such an antiphilosophy is crucial to the event that can mark the "opening of an epoch, transformation of the relations between the possible and the impossible" (45).[11] The Badiousian event names a rupture through which a truth is revealed; the person who remains militantly faithful to this truth adopts it as his or her singularity, and this is the case for Saint Paul. Such an event is not just an occurrence with powerful consequences for being, but it also disputes the very idea of being as the ground of truth procedures. Even more, it emphasizes a tautological commitment shared across particularities that particularity can no longer be the basis for identity. Paul's antiphilosophy does not systematize any truth, and indeed is allergic to specificity. Instead, it asks us to rethink the protocols of ontology. In this Pauline event, identity is no longer an additive process that increases its potency by adjectival enhancement. It becomes the minus one—that which has to be subtracted from all substance in order to qualify for the universal: a universal "[cannot] take root in the element of identity" (11). Badiou's universalism insists not on the negation of identity but on interrupting in surprising ways its inexorable march toward a preordained goal.

Such a rethinking of universalism both accords, and is at odds, with current leftist approaches to universalism. Eric Lott notes that Ernesto Laclau, for instance, "insists on the political necessity of universalism, but only as a category definitively decoupled from its classical philosophical basis.... He proposes a return to the idea in a strictly political sense that has nothing to do with the quest for Truth or a true Subject or an end of historical contradiction in the rule of a universal class" (670).[12] This "Universalism which is not One" (Linda Zerilli's term) is being actively theorized in order to recuperate one of philosophy's most reviled concepts. Even as Badiou's theory chimes with such attempts to uncouple universalism from metaphysical truth, it jars in relation to Laclau's attempt to fill the universal with different contents. Laclau argues that the erstwhile contest between particularism and universalism now takes place between various forms of particularism, each of which vies to fill the role of the universal. For instance, the specific difference of negritude can rise to the level of the universal by demanding universal human rights for all. In doing so, negritude would tap into the disenfranchisement experienced by women, homosexuals, and other minorities, and *stand in for them all*. This universal would be generated after a contest, with the understanding that next time, feminism might ascend to the level of the universal. As Laclau notes: "The place of the universal is an empty one and there is no a priori reason for it not to be filled by *any* content" (60).[13]

What marks this newer leftism is that its recuperation of universalism pivots on the notion of difference. Or rather, universalism is now being resuscitated *in the name of* difference. Universalism is expounded as a systematized philosophy of difference, unlike in Badiou, where universalism is an anti-ontology espoused by an antiphilosopher. For Laclau, particularism is reinforced rather than challenged in its reformulation as the universal. His argument empties out the finality of the universal, but immediately reassures us that it can be filled with any substantive particularity. Even Žižek, despite being a trenchant critic of the pitfalls of multiculturalism, argues that "universality is never empty; it is always coloured by some *particular* content" (110; emphasis mine).[14]

These reformulations of universalism are committed to two movements. First, emptying out the potency of the universal to mean all things at all times across all cultures and languages. And second, *filling* this newly emptied category of the universal with competing and successive differences so that the status quo cannot reenter through the back door. While I will take as instructive the insistence on emptying out the universal, I am less tempted by the rush to then fill that emptiness. Even less am I drawn to the idea that the emptiness should be filled with a notion of sexual specificity or any other particularity that might undergird universalist struggle. Instead, I want to consider what it might mean to formulate a universalism that can revolutionize the way in which we consider differences. In this I follow much more fully Žižek's challenge to theorists of the Left: "the Left has a choice today: either it accepts the predominant liberal democratic horizon (democracy, human rights and freedoms...), and engages in a hegemonic battle *within* it, *or it risks the opposite gesture of refusing its very terms, of flatly rejecting today's liberal blackmail that courting any prospect of radical change paves the way for totalitarianism*" (326).

The accusation most elicited by universalism is that of being unhistorical. Studies of politics and culture frequently oppose universalist assumptions about the world to historicist ones, where the former is understood to assume the existence of ideas and ideologies across space and time, while the latter is understood to attend to the historical specificities of the production and consumption of texts and peoples. However, as critics of historicism have increasingly been arguing, the opposition between universalism and historicism is itself false since it assumes that chronological particulars are the universal way of determining specificity. Indeed, as such critics—from Leo Bersani to Lauren Berlant—have been suggesting, the Academy's insistence on historicism has allowed a very specific form of study to become hegemonic; in other words, historicism is as universalizing as it accuses universalism of being.

Indeed, even though it seems to be recent, a radical universalism that demands a disruption of the status quo rather than simply tinkering with things the way they are is not a new idea. Badiou stands in a long line of thinkers who have sought to create something universally different rather than continue the universal regime of difference. Such a universalism is available for Badiou in Paul, and it is also present in the very Enlightenment thought that is vilified for its espousal of universalism as Reason (for Immanuel Kant) and as the progression of World Spirit (for G. W. F. Hegel). Commonly dismissed as the philosophical fount that validated colonialism and cultural oppression, the universalisms espoused by both Kant and Hegel are more radical than their European supremacist followers might have us believe. Or rather, the Enlightenment emphasis on rationality is only one way—the conservative one—in which to read these philosophers. Without detracting from the persuasiveness and historical consequence of readings that see Kant and Hegel as colonial fantasists, I would like to posit an alternative reading in which the universalism theorized during the Enlightenment hints at a fury that, when it is allowed to remain untamed, can destroy the world as we know it.

For instance, Hegel paints a provocatively frightening scenario when he imagines how universalism might entail not the creation of new knowledge but rather a pure negativity out of which emerges an anti-philosophy and an anti-ontology. While theorizing his complex notion of the will in *Elements of the Philosophy of Right*, he puts forward a profile of what he calls "one aspect of the will":

> Only *one aspect* of the will is defined here—namely this *absolute possibility of abstracting* from every determination in which I find myself or which I have posited in myself, the flight from every content as a limitation. If the will determines itself in this way, or if representational thought [*die Vorstellung*] considers this aspect in itself [*für sich*] as freedom and holds fast to it,

this is *negative* freedom or the freedom of the understanding.—This is the freedom of the void, which is raised to the status of an actual shape and passion. If it remains purely theoretical, it becomes in the religious realm the Hindu fanaticism of pure contemplation; but if it turns to actuality, it becomes in the realm of both politics and religion the fanaticism of destruction, demolishing the whole existing social order, eliminating all individuals regarded as suspect by a given order, and annihilating any organization which attempts to rise up anew. Only in destroying something does this negative will have a feeling of its own existence *[Dasein]*. It may well believe that it wills some positive condition, for instance the condition of universal equality or of universal religious life, but it does not in fact will the positive actuality of this condition, for this at once gives rise to some kind of order, a particularization both of institutions and individuals; but it is precisely through the annihilation of particularity and of objective determination that the self-consciousness of this negative freedom arises. Thus, whatever such freedom believes *[meint]* that it wills can in itself *[für sich]* be no more than an abstract representation *[Vorstellung]*, and its actualization can only be the fury of destruction.[15]

Several strains can be discerned in this powerful paragraph, the most insistent of which is the theoretical imperative of "the flight from every content as a limitation." If the will (and therefore the self) posits itself apart from limits on its substance, then it immediately opens itself and the world up to the danger of nonparticularity from which it can only be rescued by jettisoning the spirit of universalism altogether.

Let us trace this argument, which is in conversation with another train of thought in the excerpt quoted above. There is the equal dismissal of "Hindu fanaticism" and the French Revolution; if anything, the latter is criticized more trenchantly as the actualization of the unbridled will. This in turn leads to the insistence that the will without borders is dangerous; Hegel says later that the fully developed "I" is the one that has limits on its will. The particular curb rather than the unbridled exercise is what makes the will universal. So far, then, Hegel is arguing *against* what he is commonly accused of doing; instead of giving us a brief for an absolute universality, he advocates that universalism should be curbed by the particular. In this notion of absolute universalism, the universal has a specificity as its rider: Freedom of the Spirit is universal, but it can best be achieved by the German State. For Hegel, the universal *is* that which is tied to a particularity. Such a universalism—in which a specific masquerades as a universal—is, for Hegel, a positive thing that allows the world to move forward toward teleological perfection (Laclau would agree). This particular, disciplined, curbed, restrained, and rational will that rises to the category of the absolute echoes an identitarian insistence on the ontological truth of particular regimes of difference. Indeed, there is no incompatibility between this version of Hegelian universalism and current identity politics, since both insist on filling the notion of the universal with specific contents. The universalism of the German State for which Hegel is so often derided is indistinguishable from the universalism of negritude, or the universalism of sexual equality, each of which can be elevated hegemonically and teleologically as a universal that projects its particular interest in the form of the universal good.

But then there is an underbelly to this Hegelian universalism that revels in the sheer pleasure of detailing the effects of an *unbridled* will: it is a "negative ... freedom of the void" that will unleash a "fury of destruction" without leading to any synthesis whatsoever. Unbridled universalism has no positive to offer, and it is at odds with the universalism typically attributed to Hegel. It is destructive of all particulars: "It does not in fact will the positive actuality of this condition, for this at once gives rise to some kind of order, a particularization both of institutions and individuals; but it is precisely *through the annihilation of particularity* and of objective determination that the self-consciousness of this negative freedom arises" (emphasis mine). This brand of universalism does not specify contents by which to identify itself; it insists, rather, on the destruction of all contents, on dis-content. The furious universalism that Hegel outlines here—in order that it can be rejected all the more fully—is more suited to a destruction of specificities. Far from *filling* the category of the universal, this destructive universalism altogether gets rid of the regime of difference to which we are attached. Instead of replacing one cancelled specificity with a better one, it enacts something more radical in its effects.

Indeed, one can see clearly why Marx would call himself a Hegelian thinker: quite apart from his belief in a version of the Hegelian dialectic, it is the revolutionary destructiveness described above that appears in Marx's own interest in whole-scale revolution. For instance, in *The German Ideology*, Marx makes clear the nature of the Communist Revolution:

> This appropriation [of the means of production] is further determined by the manner in which it must be effected. It can only be effected through a

union, which by the character of the proletariat itself can again only be a universal one, and through a revolution, in which, on the one hand, the power of the earlier mode of production and intercourse and social organization is overthrown, and on the other hand, there develops the universal character and the energy of the proletariat, without which the revolution cannot be accomplished; and in which, further, *the proletariat rids itself of everything that still clings to it from its previous position in society.* (emphasis mine)[16]

In one of several reiterations of this notion, Marx states:

> In all revolutions up till now the mode of activity always remained unscathed and it was only a question of a different distribution of this activity, a new distribution of labour to other persons, whilst the communist revolution is directed against the preceding *mode* of activity, does away with *labour*, and abolishes the rule of all classes with the classes themselves, because it is carried through by the class which no longer counts as a class in society, is not recognised as a class, and is in itself the expression of the dissolution of all classes, nationalities, etc., within present society. . . . [T]his revolution is necessary, therefore, not only because the *ruling* class cannot be overthrown in any other way, but also because the class *overthrowing* it can only in a revolution succeed in ridding itself of all the muck of ages and become fitted to found society anew. (193)

To get rid of the cumulative, hardened accretion of the "muck of ages," Marx fully endorses the "fury of destruction" that Hegel outlines in his *Philosophy of Right.* Crucially, for Marx, getting rid of this muck involves getting rid not only of one class of people but also of *the structure of class* altogether. Previous revolutions have failed because they have never been full; at most, they have wanted to replace one class with another, or ask for better living conditions. The Communist Revolution, in contrast, would undo the entire structure of class and labor. Rather than simply challenging the mode of a specific activity, it would undo the framework within which activity and leisure are currently construed, managed, and enforced. It would not trade in half measures: complete revolution is its goal.

The labor of this revolution is universal on two fronts: first, it destroys the contents of a socioeconomic structure that generates nothing but inequality and disaffection. Far from seeking, then, to fill this structure with its own contents—for instance, with the proletariat instead of the ruling class—Marx makes it clear that the proletariat must rid itself of all that marks it as a class. The proletariat must kill itself as the proletariat in order to build a classless society. There is no other way for a full revolution to be effected. Second, the labor of the communist revolution is universal because work and workers are universal and do not belong to a particular society or country or culture: "The Communists are further reproached with desiring to abolish countries and nationality. The working men have no country. We cannot take from them what they have not got" (488). Marx's internationalism—"Workers of the world, unite!"—is a universalism of dis-contentment that undoes differences in order to deploy a sameness by which *all* are affected. For him, that sameness is oppression by the socioeconomic system of capitalism and imperialism; his manifesto for a revolution pivots on an indifference to categories of identity produced by an unjust capitalist system of production. Not difference, then, as the basis for revolution, but indifference. Not nation-states as the basis of a new regime, but the abolition of borders. Not a new structure of class, but the abandonment of class altogether. Not a polite request for accommodation, but the wholesale destruction of the "muck of ages." Not a reasoned paper about politics, but a polemical manifesto for revolt.

That this revolt can be effected most radically by a universalism whose destructive aspect is gloriously outlined and then fearfully shunned even by Hegel should allow us to use universalism, as Marx did, for its dangerous potential. Rather than recuperating universalism in the name of difference, then, I want to use universalism's fury to destroy our investment in difference as the basis of identity.

In *Saint Paul*, Badiou says that any move to collapse differences "does not permit us to lose sight of the fact that, in . . . the world *there are differences*. One can even maintain that there is nothing else" (98). For Badiou, there is no getting away from difference: it is what marks the world in which we live, and it would be foolish, not to mention futile, to ignore its presence. One cannot pretend differences do not exist. Nor can we downplay their importance to individuals as well as to structures of thought and organization. Indeed, rather than suggesting that we should ignore some differences and consolidate others so that only a few, crucial, ones remain, or that we should use differences to join rather than separate people, Badiou theorizes his move toward indifference in relation to universalism: "[I]t is imperative that universality not present itself under the aspect of particularity. Differences can be transcended only if benevolence with regard to customs and opinions presents itself as *an indifference that tolerates differences*, one whose sole material test lies . . . in being able and knowing how to practice them oneself" (99).

Badiou locates our ability to go beyond difference squarely in the self and situates universalism as being quite different from particularity. As a backdrop to this comment, Badiou quotes Paul's observation in *Corinthians* that he becomes all things to all people in order to speak to them about the universalism of the event—he becomes weak in order to speak to the weak, and strong in order to speak to the strong. Badiou's Paul addresses both Jews and Greeks, but not *as* Jews and Greeks inasmuch as those categories for him are no longer determinative of identity. Jewish law and Greek knowledge can no longer be translated into an identity that keeps apart Jews and Greeks. Universalism must be understood as the thing that can be all things to all people without being any one thing in particular to any specific person—that is the only way in which it can succeed. Compare this to the Mexican Zapatista revolutionary Subcomandante Marcos's famous response to an accusation by his right-wing opponents that he was gay: "Yes, Marcos is gay. Marcos is gay in San Francisco, Black in South Africa, an Asian in Europe, a Chicano in San Ysidro, an anarchist in Spain, a Palestinian in Israel, a Mayan Indian in the streets of San Cristobal, a Jew in Germany, a Gypsy in Poland, a Mohawk in Quebec, a pacifist in Bosnia, a single woman on the Metro at 10pm, a peasant without land, a gang member in the slums, an unemployed worker, an unhappy student and, of course, a Zapatista in the mountains."[17] The self that speaks of itself in the third person might end up reifying its self. But it can also provide the basis for a revolution in which the self becomes indifferent to itself.

Speaking of "Paul's extreme wariness with regard to every rule, every rite, that would assume the form of universal militantism by making of it a bearer of differences and particularities in turn" (99–100), Badiou points out that it is only in individually being able to traverse differences that one can hope to prise other people's grip from their specificities. Or rather, traversing differences while in the grip of the universal models a way of being in which people need not give up the differences by which they function in the world while *at the same time* appreciating the universal that asks them to transcend those boundaries as identity. The individual thus remains an individual marked by race, class, gender, culture, even as s/he decides to give up being grounded in any one of those markers. This is less a matter of conscious choice (both "conscious" and "choice" are socially and ideologically overdetermined terms) made in the face of other choices, and more a description of the ways in which we already live. We already know how to be indifferent and how to live in difference, but we have been encouraged to forget those modes of being. An indifferent universalism allows us to undo the incentives we have been given to forget those ways. Embracing the universal does not ask for the sacrifice of the particular but only an indifference to it. Far from telling us to ignore ontological categories, universalism demands that we acknowledge the fact of our restless movement among them.

This indifference to particularity is also a part of what Marx envisages in the Communist utopia:

> As soon as the distribution of labour comes into being, each man has a particular, exclusive sphere of activity, which is forced upon him and from which he cannot escape. He is a hunter, a fisherman, a shepherd, or a critical critic, and must remain so if he does not want to lose his means of livelihood; while in communist society, where nobody has one exclusive sphere of activity but each can become accomplished in any branch he wishes, society regulates the general production and thus makes it possible for me to do one thing today and another tomorrow, to hunt in the morning, fish in the afternoon, rear cattle in the evening, criticise after dinner, just as I have a mind, *without ever becoming hunter, fisherman, shepherd or critic.* (160; emphasis mine)

Despite the specific use of the masculine pronoun here, Marx outlines a world in which specificity would not attach to any single person. His version of universalism does not destroy specific professions, but it allows us to traverse them without settling on any one in particular. Such dilettantism becomes a bad thing under capitalism, where it is imperative to specialize in order to be more productive (even if you change professions, as is increasingly the norm, you cannot simultaneously pursue many since the assumption is that you will work sixteen-hour days in whatever job you are doing at the moment). But for Marx, it is important that specificity not be allowed to mark one's identity either in relation to one's self or in relation to the other. A universal is both everything and nothing at once—it is to be weak with the weak and strong with the strong—and it allows us to collapse differences without getting rid of, or dis-acknowledging, them altogether. Differences will continue to exist but will lose their power to define.

Thus, even as he acknowledges the proliferation and importance of differences, Badiou insists that the universal cannot be formulated as a *version* of the particular—universalism is not particularism on steroids. Instead, he advocates indifference. Despite conjuring up a shrug of the shoulders, or even political apathy, indifference is not about heartlessness or ignorance. Rather, it names an anti-ontological state of being that would acknowledge and embody difference without becoming that difference. A state of indifference would interrupt the line that automatically connects soma with self or dress with identity or opinion with body. We will be able to encounter, for instance, a woman without already knowing what it means for her to be a woman and already assuming that she wants to belong to any definition of "woman" with which we have been supplied. "Assume nothing" is an early slogan of gay activists in the United States; indifference makes good on that phrase. The politics of indifference would support activisms, but not ones that invest in the ontology of difference. Rather than being hemmed in by difference—single or multiple—that can be signified in advance, indifference is attuned to a universality of difference in which specific differences cannot be used as the basis of stable signification. In an indifferent world, an organization of subaltern scholars would not include people only working on India; a march to protest sexual violence would attack the structural framework of gender and sexual orientation; a symposium on race would put pressure on the assignment of color and character to somatic bodies. Instead of echoing structures of power that are exclusionary, a political activism based on indifference would challenge them.

Indeed, the specific thrust of indifference for Badiou is that identity cannot be used as the basis on which to formulate universalism. Rather than elevating one's particular difference as the one that matters, indifference treats as infinitely traversable the boundaries among peoples, places, and things, and does not prescribe which belongs to who or what. This infinite traversal does not mean differences don't exist or that contingent material circumstances do not make them nontraversable in the moment, simply that differences cannot become, obsessively, the basis on which to formulate and navigate the truth of identity. Universalism thus does not consist of everyone sounding the same at all times—we might consider this the American melting-pot model in which no matter from where immigrants come, the goal is to end up speaking with an "American" accent. Universalism does not mandate sameness nor does it use difference as the basis for identity. Rather, it involves the recognition that difference itself is universal and therefore unremarkable.

To return to the incident with which I began, it is easy to see how the immigration officer's response, based as it was on a polite adherence to difference, would have changed had he been acting indifferently. In response to my answer that I teach English, he would have asked me *what* I taught, or even what constitutes the teaching of English, rather than presuming that I worked on Naipaul and Rushdie. My answer would still have involved a particular author—Shakespeare—but it would not have been an answer that either conformed to or departed from a fixed sense of difference. Indifferently, he would not have presumed to know what I work on and would have appreciated the imaginative leaps that mark so many of us in our choice of profession and lifestyle. He would have allowed the idea of difference to interrupt his assumed sense of cultural, sexual, social, gendered, differences. The difference that disrupts the discourse of differences no longer performs the ontological division mandated by the term. Instead, it becomes indifference. Difference asks us to abide by the constraints of its agenda, while indifference does not require any adherence whatsoever. Instead, indifference allows us to travel without asking for a visa to authenticate the legality of our desire.

Badiou suggests in his study of Paul that "the universal is not the negation of particularity. It is the measured advance across a distance relative to perpetually subsisting particularity" (110). Even as differences exist, they cannot be translated into particular identities. Differences are way stations but never destinations; indeed, universalism is a movement across these way stations that does not arrive at an ontological resting place. At a time when a lot of money and intellectual energy is being spent on assuring people that their difference *is* their identity and they should remain circumscribed within it, Badiou's intervention seems startling. Far from either mandating the suspension of difference or advocating for a specific difference, he refuses to validate differences of dress or religion or ethnicity or language as being entirely determinative of anything, let alone of the self. Instead, he suggests we should develop an indifference to difference in which differences in and of themselves become neither instigators to crime nor upholders of uniqueness. An attitude of indifference would remove the sense of ownership over moral propriety that is the basis for much of the violence in the world today. It would allow us to undo the burden of identitarian specificity that prompts brutal actions every day. Arguably, identity has caused more damage in the world than not, which makes our attachment to it all the more unfathomable. Indifference to identity might allow us to counter some of that physical and conceptual violence. As part of this counterprocedure, Badiou notes that there is "an essential link between the 'for all' of the universal and the 'without cause'" (77). By undoing causality, universalism both allows connections to travel in unexpected directions and disables a structure in which one particular can be valorized over another as being more consequential.

Queer Universalism

How can an indifferent universalism be lived? One answer to this question is that we already live it. None of us is ever reducible to any one of our selves, and each of us stretches against identitarian constraints all the time. But this is true only because of the role that desire plays in our lives. Desire is that which in every instance hollows out ontology. Whether it is libidinal desire for someone who falls outside the bounds of what we consider "our" sexuality, or a longing that stretches beyond the borders of our politics, desire does not respect limits. It is restless and nonunifying. It keeps moving, which is why it disables ontological fixes. And it is indifferent, which is why it is politically incorrect. Desire is surprising because it can erupt at the most unexpected moments and in the most inconvenient circumstances. Perhaps most important, desire cannot suture bodies onto identities; it fails to arrest its metonymic slide with the fiction of a unified self. Fanon's Antillean boy, we remember, is oppressed precisely when his fantasy of desire is fixed to a somatic body, and the unity of body and desire is given back to him as his identity. Desire is too fickle to be contained by any one theoretical idiolect, which is why its only theoretical companion is universalism. An indifferent universalism allows us to theorize a radical politics of desire, a queer universalism.[18]

Indeed, desire is crucial to thinking about universalism not because it will set us free but because we cannot know what it will do. If (1) the ontological grounding of difference ignores the lived realities of our lives, and (2) these lived realities allow us to note the universal inadequacy of differences, then (3) desire undergirds the restless indifference that refuses to settle into ontological certainty. A universalism that does not itself have an identity—it is indifferent to difference—is marked by and modeled on a desire that traverses boundaries without positing an identity for itself. If indifference is an acknowledgment of our universal failure to occupy an identity, then desire demonstrates that failure by straying continually from its perch of seeming fixity. This failure is also the success of our unontologizable being in the world. Desire is universally indifferent and this indifferent desire marks us all.

As such a formulation suggests, desire is fundamental to the idea and project of universalism. The job of a universal indifference is to uncouple desire from the clutches of the law of particularity because desire universally exceeds the particular even as it is marked by it—an indifferent desire limns a superabundance that is always in excess of its particularities.[19] To push this point even further, desire attaches to individual bodies and figures and ideas, but it also moves through and beyond them into a realm of perpetual dis-content. Desire is empty, temporarily filled, and then emptied again. This does not mean that people do not follow the trajectory, say, of heterosexual desire, for their entire lives, or that they do not stay with one partner for life. But to admit as much is to recognize only the identitarian apparatus within which desire has been trapped; it does not mean forgetting the excessiveness of desire even and especially when we might not act on it. Far from expecting desire to render ontology, then, we need to realize that ontology is always a fabrication that uses desire as its crutch. Desire changes whether or not we act on those changes. Specificity only *seems* to be a resting place: if we no longer perform an ontological calculation that anchors desire in identity, then we can also practice an indifference that, for Paul, refuses to ontologically ground either Jew or Greek.

I will term such an indifferent universalism "queer" not because it has to do with an identity we can understand as queer, but precisely because, like universalism, queerness too is marked by a desire that refuses the contours of a fixed body.[20] Far from inhabiting gay or straight bodies—as though object choice could render desire legible—we are all marked by a superabundance of desire that might be termed queer.[21] Such is the mundane radicalism of queer desire that it simply (and often blindly or non-self-reflexively) desubjectivizes all categories of identity grounded in sexual specificity. This superabundance refuses to give us an identity even as we are busy tying it down to different bodies. Such a refusal is also very much our lived experience. Multiple marriages; gay men who were once straight; straight women who were once lesbians; flirtations; polygamy; polyandry; bisexuality; transgender; eunuchs; polyamory. Even as desire is made to define "one," no one's desire can be contained by a single epithet, or even by a series of epithets: we are different combinations at different moments, all of which add up to a subtraction of specificity. Desire resides in us, but with scant regard for who we are. Far from being a touchy-feely claim about multiplicity and difference, such a realization empties us of a specificity that can be herded into a categorical difference. If we take seriously the universal queerness of desire, then we lose the particularity of the queer body and our belief in its existence.[22] Queer universalism can only ever be indifferent to difference.

The difficulty in being able to decipher the meaning of desire in advance is precisely the ethical claim of a queer politics outlined by Eve Kosofsky Sedgwick. Indeed, her majoritarian reading of desire suggests it is "an unpredictably powerful solvent of stable identities" (85); this is what Jonathan Goldberg has described as Sedgwick's "queer universalism" (72).[23] As opposed to lesbian and gay identities, and the identities contained in acronyms of increasing length, queerness posits only a horizon of its own impossibility.[24] The answer to the question of what *is* queer cannot zero in on a set of visible or embodied differences that mark people or events as queer—it is not a difference that can stand as an identity.[25] By showcasing a desire that does not allow for any particular identity, universalism not only announces itself as queer—*empty of content, revolutionary, indifferent*— but it also argues that queerness is universal. Queerness refuses to settle in a country or language or color or dress or gender. A queer universalism does not assign any positive content to the term "queer": it is not an additive concept in which queerness is *added* to make a more robust universalism. Rather, queer universalism gathers together particularities *across* so-called identities, and refuses to identify queerness in any particularity. In direct contrast to the *additive* impulse of particularity, an indifferent universalism breaks free of a predicative anchor. Unlike the empty signifier of a universalism continually *filled* with competing particularities, queerness neither claims to be particular, nor does it ask that universalism be filled. Insisting instead on the particularity of a desire whose reach is universal, queerness refuses the communitarian project of formulating collectivities and affirms, instead, the inextricability of queerness from the project of subjectivization. As such, queer universalism pushes at the boundaries of identity-specific fields that presume a stable process of subject-formation. Even those scholars devoted to exploring the intersections among various subjects often do so by respecting the categorical imperatives of each subfield, but queer universalism intends no such respect. Indeed, it seeks to explore a nonfoundationalism that takes queerness seriously enough to resist being

sutured to any one particular subject or identity. In opposition to the additive properties of LGBT studies, for instance, queer universalism under-
takes the refusal of identity outlined by Lee Edelman when he notes that
"queerness can never define an identity; it can only ever disturb one" (17).
The negation insisted upon by Edelman's queerness is Badiou's universal.

Indeed, what is universally queer is the ontological impossibility of self-
identity. Everything is queer because no-thing—peoples, events, desires—
can achieve ontological wholeness. Our current political dispensations per-
sist in positing the particular integrity of an entity as its most pressing
characteristic, but there is not a single particularity that is unique. What
remains *singular*, however, is this nonfixity of the particular. Particulars
do not add up to identities: identity is universally more than the sum of its
parts and therefore universally less than a solid ontology. What is universal
about desire is the failure to rein it in. It would thus be a mistake to assume
that desire is simply liberatory and that an indifferent desire will always
be radical. If anything, the most characteristic feature of desire is that one
cannot know what it will do. It can underwrite conservative politics—
witness the agitation for gay marriage. And it can break with convention
so entirely as to leave one breathless—witness the women who walk out
of arranged marriages to be with other women. It is precisely this unpre-
dictability that makes it impossible to harness desire for prescriptive use.
Desire can only ever be descriptive—we can note its ebbs and flows, its
fluctuations, its restlessness—but we can never predict any of its movements. Desire moves—that is its only strategy—and it moves beyond sexual desire into imaginative desires of all kinds; we may desire to belong to
a different race or a different nation or a different gender, to speak a different language. All movement is marked by desire, no matter where that
movement might go. And all movements of desire depend on an indifference to difference. This is why desire cannot be used to undergird an ontological notion of difference—because it does not stick around for long
enough to give identity its imprimatur. Desire moves universally; it is indifferent to bodies and colors and genitalia, not because one cannot be and
is not attracted to specific bodies but because those specificities do not add
up to an identity. It is increasingly difficult to tell the difference between a
dildo and a penis, a vagina and an asshole, a man and a woman, and even if
it were not, one would rarely pass a blind test that mapped desire neatly onto
a specific body. Equally, it is easy for nonpartisans to hear Hindi and Urdu
coexisting, Irish- and Boston-accented English sharing a similar palate,

and Burmese mingling with Thai. Desire moves; whether or not we overtly follow along in its wake, it tugs us in so many directions that there is no "us" that can survive its vertiginous moves and countermoves.

Queer universalism, then, is indifferent to ontology—it does not give us particular identities, considering instead *all* identities as not fully determined, or knowable, in short, as queer.[26] Unlike the so-called postracial, postgender, postgay trends of our own times, indifference insists on seeing and noting difference everywhere. Indeed, its political compulsion derives from observing the multiple differences within which we live, the countless differences we create, and the many differences that define our lives. But far from solidifying identity, these multiple differences offer instead a gap between difference and identity. Such an undoing of the ontological basis of the self is not simply an experiment to come up with a better version of the self—that formulation would be condemned to remain within the realm of a liberal voluntarism. Rather, interrupting the line of identity—as I wanted to do with my immigration officer—advocates a radical refusal of ontology. This refusal makes manifest the workings of desire. And it lays bare the superabundant longing that is the very stuff of queer universalism.

For Badiou, universalism is founded on an *event* that disrupts the protocols of ontology. But what, one might ask, would constitute the event of queerness? Far from being an actual event (my encounter at the immigration counter), mythological or historical, that takes place at an actual moment in time, an event is a horizon of theoretical possibility, a point of saturation at which something snaps, allowing reformulations of ontology and epistemology; an event is that which interrupts the repetitions that we term knowledge.[27] Despite his insistence on the fictional nature of the resurrection, however, Badiou tethers the event to the resurrection of Christ. Thus, even as Badiou says that the object of Paul's militant fidelity (i.e., the miracle of the Incarnation) is unimportant, the very title of his book suggests that Badiou's universalism slides into a Christian particularism. Such a particularism would be impossible for queer universalism. Since queer universalism can and does travel, it becomes unrooted in Western Christianity; it becomes, one might say, indifferent to it. The event does not mark a specific chronological moment or occupy a particular historical or spatial location; it can refer to a theoretical process of reconsideration that asks questions about what counts as identity and its relation to lived experience. Inevitably, such an inquiry will take place in concert with others over long periods of time and across national, cultural, social, sexual, boundaries.

A universal destabilizing of ontology need not be tied to a specific occasion even as it might erupt more fully at certain pressure points than at others. The event of queerness would thus be nothing more or less than a challenge to the ontological grounding of desire and politics. Such an event shares with a Derridean *différance* the emptying-out of the ontological particulars of a self. But even more, it provides the ground from which to deal with the effects of such an emptying-out. It allows us to acknowledge the impossibility of identity and enables us to live with that impossibility. A queer event is both Derridean and Maoist—it is theory *as* praxis.

And this praxis is both structural and individual. No matter what our individual degrees of access to power and wealth may be, we are all trapped within ontological constraints in which individuality is an effect rather than a cause of power. As such, neither wealth nor poverty automatically predisposes us to accept or resist the idea of an indifferent universalism. Indeed, one must insist that poverty is no deterrent to an unfixed ontology; often the very opposite is true because there is less status quo to be protected. Equally, though, a poor person might choose to identify with the wealthy and turn her back on anticapitalistic errancy. We simply do not know which way desiring fantasies will go, and there is no point in legislating for that. Desire is not liberatory, and fantasy can tend toward political conservatism; a woman, for instance, might derive great pleasure from being dominated sexually by a man. But queer universalism is not about the ethics of desire—it does not separate out the good from the bad desire. Instead, it asks us to recognize the impossibility of recognizing desire with any finality. The woman who likes to be sexually dominated by a man might be his boss in the workplace. What, then, does that make her? What is her identity? Desire allows us to be indifferent to a regime of difference in which a body can be fixed in an identitarian register. We would no longer be surprised, for instance, by the homosexual desires of a straight man, or the linguistic fluency of a lower-caste person, or the Shakespearean pretensions of an un-Englishwoman, or the nonwhiteness of an Englishman. Equally, we could allow ourselves to be surprised by the unexpected turns that desire takes in the world. Queer universalism articulates a politics of nonontology in which superabundance is only artificially fixed in place and the artifice should not itself be confused with fixity. Every identity is excessive because each one could belong to any number of people, and potentially to us all. Equally, none of them belongs to any of us. This is a description of the way in which we actually live.

But the question that these formulations beg is about agency. What is the ontological status of the event, of queerness, of indifference? Is there a "one" that opts for these things? Is it a choice to disregard identity? If so, then who gets to make that choice? Is it simply bad faith not to disregard it? These questions acknowledge the problem with assuming that queerness is a matter of individual choice. Indeed, indifference must not be watered down to an anodyne liberalism that insists one can be whatever one "chooses" to be. Instead, theorizing the queer event allows us to foreground the *structural* nature of indifference rather than making it only an option for individuals either to accept or decline. When I argue, therefore, that our identity is not fixed, I am accounting for a universal structure that is the failure of identity. Even those who believe that identity is fixed and knowable do not believe themselves to be unchanging; they simply ignore the changes and fix on one difference as their identity. By understanding identity as a structural construct without content, indifference refuses to reduce desire to a matter of "choice." It insists, rather, that choice is itself a fully loaded term, and so long as our only choice is between a binary— identity or indifference—it is not a choice at all. Instead it is a continued imprisonment in the jail of identities predicated on differences.

Equally, however, structure cannot determine our place in the world. After all, not everyone who belongs to a particular class or a particular gender behaves *in the same way*. That is, of course, the assumption we are encouraged to make when we are told to adopt an identity in opposition to another identity. But such an assumption is both patronizing and untrue; it is created in order to maximize resources for one group *as opposed to* another. Instead, we make choices all the time even when those choices might not appear to be chosen. Should we conform or not? Whom do we desire? Should we acquiesce in oppression or speak out against it? The choice, therefore, is not *between* structure and consciousness; rather, indifference suggests that we are all continually in play between choice and structure. Queer universalism inclines toward Marx's brilliant dictum that people make their own history but not in circumstances of their own choosing.[28] Acknowledging indifference as being the stuff of our lived realities involves negotiating many structures, but it is also a decision that each of us makes to exit a fantasy of identitarian coherence. What's even more difficult than effecting this exit is doing it in the knowledge that exiting the fantasy of identity does not guarantee entry into another, better fantasy termed indifference. Queer universalism is not about a liberal voluntarism that allows the best of us to exit bad categories and join better ones. Rather, the argument about indifference is an argument about refusal without certain gain. We refuse to ignore the way we already live. We refuse to buy into the shining structures of categorical identity. We refuse to ignore the violence of difference. We refuse the ontological goal of differences. We refuse to reduce indifference to callousness. And we refuse to ignore the flexible fickleness of desire.

What makes universalism universal, then, is not its content but its mode of refusal. If we do not choose to be indifferent, then we are also choosing—in circumstances, perhaps, not of our making—not to refuse. Dismissing the idea that universalism is always a particularity, Badiou emphasizes that "every particularity is a conformation, a conformism. It is a question of maintaining a nonconformity with regard to that which is always conforming us" (110). Universalism thus argues for a wholesale revision of cultural-political-social-sexual habitation through an indifference that is itself the detritus of a queer event.

Let us term this queer event, this event of queerness, this space and time of nonconformity, this sphere of nonontology, the theater. Not a literal theater, necessarily, nor even a performative one in the Butlerian sense, but an evental one that stages the impossibility of ontology. Suggesting that embodiment refuses self-presence, and desire moves freely among characters, theater showcases the recalibration of identity as indifference. In different modes, indifference reimagines interpersonality as impersonation, as a serial constitution of selves that are transient and nonessential. It plays out the decimating effects of desire on identity, and it enacts the universal pleasures of nonconformity. Such indifference is theatrical in several ways—it is performative without positing an essence, interactive without implying sociality, and pleasurable without suggesting identity. It is a negative space inasmuch as it does not present us with "real" people. And perhaps most important, it is a space in which actors must project their desire into the unknown in order to connect with it most fully. Theatrical desire is about the inevitability of extension into space and time and the vicissitudes of that extension. A theatrical indifference acts out the universality of a desire that belongs to all and is owned by none. It showcases a universal structure in which an ontological self is wrecked by desire's unrelenting stride.

Such an investment in the queer event of theater is also polemical since it radically undresses what we commonly understand by desire and the self that owns it. The polemic is a queer genre not only because it is often derided for being too unruly but also because it does not respect the kinds of boundaries and parameters by which more traditional monographs might be governed. Instead, what follows in this book are theatrical tales of travel and dramatized travelers' tales. These tales span geography, chronology, genre, and language, demanding neither customs nor immigration clearance, traveling at will, for instance, from Nigeria to England, traveling with will in Shakespearean drama, traveling will-fully between languages that have long been divided from one another and histories that have long been declared distinct.[29] Every chapter showcases—as history, as performance, as narrative tradition—a desire in which movement is paramount and indifference to difference essential. Universally, across time and space, they suggest we need to undo our protocols of knowing and being. Queerly, across texts and desires, they insist we develop an indifference to difference that will allow us to live in difference differently.[30]

1 Out of Africa

Yinka Shonibare's Museum of Desire

But first, what does it mean to live *in* difference? While in New Zealand a few summers ago, I was given a glowing report of an exhibition that had passed through Auckland from Sydney and had just set sail for the United States. It was a multimedia exhibition, featuring sculptures, films, paintings, photographs, and installations, all of which challenged the boundaries around bodies and interrogated the assumptions we have about identity. In fact, the artist was quoted as saying that "[he is interested in] the possibility of adopting a stance that questions not only the status quo but [also our] own assumptions about that status quo."[1] And then I was told that his exhibition would be shown at the National Gallery of African Art in Washington, D.C.

Because I had already started thinking about questions of particularity and universalism, my first thought was this: If the artist is interested in complicating identity, then why show him in a museum that announces its identitarian difference? Does the setting assume that the artist is African? Does the artist himself lay claim to that identity? *Can* he lay claim to any one identity if he wants to challenge its regime? The artist I am speaking of is Yinka Shonibare MBE, most often described as "a British-born Nigerian artist." His chosen name announces itself as a title. The "Yinka Shonibare" seems decidedly un-British, while the "MBE," standing as it does for a Member of the British Empire, is quintessentially so. The artist's name itself is a work of art that eludes easy fixing. At first sight, the name appeared Japanese to me, with the MBE being pronounced as "imbé." And then I thought it might be Taiwanese, like "Ng," and pronounced "bay" with a silent M; either way I was convinced the artist was East Asian. But when I found out that Yinka Shonibare MBE is an émigré Nigerian in London, and that what I was reading as the last name were the initials of the "honor" bestowed upon him by the Queen of England, that information raised a whole new set of questions. Is Shonibare a subject or object of empire? Is he British or not? Why use a title as a last name? Does that make the name a title or the title a name? Is the MBE serious, comic, or, most unreadable of all, ironic? Yinka Shonibare MBE's name entails a clash of locally legible particularities that fail to signify straightforwardly or monolithically. Like his art, which most often features headless Enlightenment dandies wearing seemingly African clothes, Yinka Shonibare MBE is hard to read.

However, even as the name and oeuvre of the artist are devoted to complicating identity, the machine of the identitarian market slots him into the museum of "African Art." In the best-case scenario, the exhibition venue in Washington might be a description of Shonibare's *art*, which, a curator could argue, is "African" in its concerns since some of his installations speak powerfully to the colonial carving up of Africa by the European powers in the nineteenth century (see his dramatic *Scramble for Africa* [2003], for example). But his work seems at least as concerned with questions of aesthetics, sexuality, and disability, to name only a few. Instead of setting up a contest among these concerns—that is, instead of organizing these artistic preoccupations hierarchically—one might still be able to ask how one trait among many gets elevated to the position of standing in synecdochally for all the others. How, for instance, does the decision get taken to show Shonibare in the Museum of African Art rather than, say, in the Museum of Desire? This is clearly a rhetorical question since there *is* no Museum of Desire anywhere in the world. Even if there were to be such a museum, it would have a difficult time determining who would and would not belong in its catalogue of exhibitions. But Shonibare's skin color seems like a clear determinant of identity, and therefore his art is displayed in the Museum of African Art. Yinka Shonibare is black and grew up for part of his life in Lagos. But whether that makes him, let alone his art, African, or even Nigerian, is one of the questions this chapter will consider.

If anything, Yinka Shonibare MBE has often been criticized for not being African "enough." He says he has "sometimes felt pressure to 'be black' in his work—a stereotyped blackness, based on notions of the primitive and the exotic."[2] For instance, his tutor at college in London in the mid-1980s once asked him why he was working on perestroika rather than something

"authentically" African. This all-too familiar demand for nativistic authenticity is often the consequence of a well-meaning desire for "multiculturalism" that ignores the ways in which its demand ossifies cultures as individual
before allowing them entry into the realm of the multicultural. The multiplicity allegedly celebrated by multiculturalism is rather a specificity that
needs to be detailed in advance of admission to the multicultural club. The
requirement for entry thus seems to cancel out the ostensible purpose of
the multicultural project itself. Indeed, one of Shonibare's responses to his
tutor's question serves to highlight the ridiculousness of the status quo
that drives the demand for authenticity: he wondered how many of his
British fellow students had been asked to paint morris dancers since that
was the only thing he could think of as authentically British. This experience seems to have been pivotal for Shonibare's art, most of which is
devoted to challenging the logic of identitarian authenticity and wondering if identity is ever available as a pure category. His conclusion, amply
documented in his art, is that "all culture is essentially hybrid, and . . . the

Figure 1. Yinka Shonibare, *Scramble for Africa*, 2003. Copyright Yinka Shonibare. Courtesy
The Pinnell Collection, Dallas; Commissioned by the Museum for African Art, New York

notion of purity is null and void."[3] Shonibare notes that "there is a way in which one is perceived, and there's no getting away from it. And I realized that if I didn't deal with it, I would just be described forever as a black artist who doesn't make work about being black. . . . I realized what I'd really have to deal with was the construction of stereotypes, and that's what my work would be about."[4]

Who or what is an African, and what is African art? These are questions that Yinka Shonibare has had to deal with repeatedly. If identity depends, as Shonibare suggests, on the ways in which we are perceived by others, then on what is that perception based? In Shonibare's case, as in almost every case, perceptions about identity seem to depend on skin color. What we look like—skin color, and also gender presentation—determines our identity. Equally, who we look at (men looking at men or women, women looking at men or women) generates sexual identity. The visual register anchored in the body is the basis for the generation of identitarian ontology. In a culture of such overwhelming visuality, the brilliance of Shonibare's art lies not only in challenging the regime of visual meaning-production, but also in asking us to interrupt the process by which a particular image gets encoded and decoded in automatic ways. This is why, for Shonibare, ethnicity and desire are bound up together—not because the two are identical, but because both race and sexuality are forms of identity that base themselves firmly in and on the body. Both cater to the privilege accorded to the visual: race responds to the prompt of what we look like, and sexuality to who we look at. Both give us a physical presence in which to anchor our assumptions about a self. And both give us the boundaries within which that self is to be contained.

Thus the figure of the dandy, whom Shonibare calls the "outsider," and who disturbs the visual logic of the body by re-creating it in unexpected ways, is a recurring motif in his work. The dandy—sexually indeterminate because usually a man calling attention to his body rather than keeping it under wraps—is also for that reason unreadable. He dresses *too* well, which makes his identity suspect and unfixable. Dandyism unsettles the binary of hetero- and homo- by focusing on a seemingly immaterial component of identity—the clothes one wears. Ironically, this immaterial component is based on the most beautiful of materials; dandyism insists that what one looks like depends on one's clothes rather than on one's skin color. By dressing "incongruously"—not befitting time or place or class or gender or caste—the dandy unsettles the straight line from skin color to identity by forcing our gaze to rest on the clothes he wears. Such narcissistic dandyism struts its stuff in Shonibare's work, from his mannequins to his films, and from his photographs to his installations.

In his 2001 photographic rendition of Oscar Wilde's *Portrait of Dorian Gray*, Shonibare produces eleven black-and-white photographs and one color picture to celebrate the dandy. Yinka Shonibare MBE himself plays Dorian amid an all-white cast in the eleven photos. But there is one color shot, which reproduces the moment in the novel when Dorian looks at the portrait; here, Shonibare has a photo of himself looking at his reflection in a mirror (Figure 2). The reflection is disfigured, but we cannot tell if the face looking into the mirror is as well. Why is this photo in color, and what is the moral of this picture fable? That narcissism distorts? That an investment in one's own image corrupts the purity of the self? Or can we think of it rather as a set of genuine questions that echoes also what Wilde is asking in his novel: How do we see ourselves in the mirror? How do we see others in the mirror? Do we ever have access to a face, or do we always

Figure 2. Yinka Shonibare, *Dorian Gray* (detail), 2001. Copyright Yinka Shonibare. Courtesy the artist and Stephen Friedman Gallery, London

only have an image? Even more pressingly, given both Shonibare's politics and his reception in the world, do we always see a black face as being disfigured? Or does the disfiguration lie in the fact that Shonibare has taken his place in Wilde's work? Does Dorian's coded homosexuality transition here into Yinka's seemingly straightforward blackness? And if so, then does that reiterate or scramble our visual and bodily codes of identity? Is homosexuality a mark that can be seen, like blackness seems to be? Or is blackness invisible, like homosexuality seems to be?[5]

Who better than Wilde to ask these questions? And who better than Shonibare to address them? The black homosexual in this photograph may not "actually" be black—perhaps the blackness is a sign only of his depravation and is something fairly recent? And he may not even be homosexual— perhaps we are only layering disease onto depravity? No matter how we look at this photograph, we are aware of the fact that we are reading it amid confused signals. Is this Dorian or not? If it is, then was Dorian actually black? The confusion of the literal and metaphorical registers (black skin or black soul?) lends a profusion of significatory possibilities to this photograph. In contrast to Shonibare's usual colorful mode, here the figure is dressed only in black and white. This starkness is both an acknowledgment of the black-and-white photos that make up the remainder of the series and a nod to the dominant visual registers in which race gets coded. Even more, the photo substitutes for the profusion of colors an excess of signification. This excess is what, in the final analysis, makes the photograph dandy—we don't know how to read it. What is the event staged by this photograph, and how does it present its desire? Such a conversation— about excess, signification, desire, and color (in every sense of the word)— is Shonibare's continual staging ground; it is his queer theory.

Indeed, conversation itself is interpreted by Shonibare in the meaning of its noun form as "sexual intercourse or intimacy."[6] He uses this sense of sexual intimacy as the backdrop against which to set an elaborate installation titled *Gallantry and Criminal Conversation* (2002), which plays with the Victorian euphemism of describing adultery as "criminal conversation." Made up of "five works that contain mature content and are not suitable for all audiences," *Gallantry and Criminal Conversation* traces the path of the Grand Tour that English gentlemen of means undertook in the seventeenth, eighteenth, and nineteenth centuries to Italy and France in order to get a flavor of Europe and become cosmopolitan citizens of the world. The Grand Tour is here imagined as tourism of a different kind as eleven life-sized mannequins engage in a set of sexual expeditions. From cunnilingus to fellatio, vaginal to anal to oral sex, this installation covers almost all the delights sex has to offer. The Grand Tour in Shonibare's hands becomes a tour both of the metropolis and the provinces of the body, and an exhibition of the sexual pleasures yielded by different erogenous zones. Accompanying each set of mannequins is a traveling case—battered, beaten, dusty—that stands witness to the distances covered by the traveler. And hanging above them all is a carriage—the ubiquitous symbol of genteel travel in Victorian England—whose wheels have allowed the mannequins their chance to journey sexually.

Desire travels; it demands extension into space and time. And travel involves both movement and, etymologically, travail or work. This travail, as the word itself suggests, is not always a pleasant or liberating experience. Not only can travel be conservative—several people travel in order to have their desires and identities confirmed rather than questioned—but it can also be fraught with dangers of disease and death. *Gallantry and Criminal Conversation* refuses to draw a line around desire—it is a sprawling and unbounded installation—and it also refuses to comfort us with scenes of safety and legibility. Instead it asks us to decode what we are seeing and challenges us to convert traveling desire into ontological identity. Desire travels—if there is one thing that it does, then that is it. Nothing more can be said with certainty about it. Desire travels, and it creates all the discomfort and disease associated with travel. It also generates all the excitement and ecstasy that accompanies travelers. Shonibare's installation depicts the criminality of desire and captures both these senses without adjudicating between them. In his work, desire is, to use Georg Lukács's term, "transcendental homelessness"—it travels and never settles and is sublime in its restlessness.[7] This is how it can disrupt the straight line by which ontology is projected onto identity. When Shonibare stands up to speak, his body is presumed to identify him as a black African—with all the assumptions that go along with it. But his art unsettles identitarian knowledge of all kinds, making former certainties uncertain.

It is the seeming fixity of the visual register—its resistance to travel—that Shonibare's art insists we resist. When asked about the politics and aesthetics of his representations in a 1996 interview, Shonibare said: "*Ceci n'est pas une pipe* by Magritte, is important for understanding my work. You know how he presents a pipe and then says it is not a pipe. You can't smoke it. Sometimes people confuse representation for what it represents.

Figure 3. Yinka Shonibare, *Gallantry and Criminal Conversation*, 2002. Copyright Yinka Shonibare. Courtesy the artist, Stephen Friedman Gallery, London and James Cohan Gallery, New York

But they are not that physical thing, *they don't exist in the world in that way*. So if you see a woman walking down a road and she's wearing African cloth, you might think—now there's African-ness, true Africanity. But that cloth, those clothes, are not African-ness."[8] While pointing to the gap between representation and self, identity and desire, Shonibare makes the crucial point that the woman dressed in African cloth, walking down the road, does not "exist in the world in that way"—she must not ontologically be confused for and as the fabric on her body because identity in fact does not work in such a straight line. Asking us to question the "proof" of what we see, Shonibare presses for a mode of disbelief that does not seek after authenticity. He emphasizes the sensual pleasure of the fabric with which he clothes his mannequins—the same fabric worn by the woman who walks down the road in his example. If we allow our eye to take in the fabric, both its aesthetics and its history, then we might not demand an authentic identity with which to match the cloth.

The conceit behind many of Shonibare's paintings, sculptures, and installations, this so-called African cloth is frequently worn and taken these days as a sign of African authenticity. Having traced the history of this cloth, however, Shonibare has found that this supposedly "African" fabric, better known as Dutch Wax Cloth (and actually termed "Real Dutch"), was manufactured by the colonial Dutch in imitation of Indonesian batiks and then sold to the Dutch West African colonies in the nineteenth century when the cloth failed to sell in southeast Asia. Produced as a copy of Indonesian batik and then rejected in Indonesia for being of inferior quality, this cloth was off-loaded in West Africa so the Dutch imperialists could recoup their imminent losses. The trajectory of the cloth—from Holland (inspired by Indonesia) via Indonesia to West Africa—militates against anchoring it in any one region or culture. This marker of African authenticity does not provide a causal link between Africa and the cloth; or between the body and the cloth in which that body is wrapped; or between the way in which the body looks and its identity. Shonibare's bodies—both the ones he makes and the one he embodies—do not, in his words, "exist in that way": they can never be singular and authentic, never be taken as a true representative of the tribe. Dutch Wax Cloth is West African; Holland is Indonesia is Africa. This is both an accurate depiction of colonial history and also exemplary of a rampant globalization that sows inequities in its wake. But it is also a challenge to unthink the limits placed on us by the geographical and conceptual borders that are the true heritage of colonialism. It is an invitation to undo some of the violence created by a colonial system in which geographical and political boundaries were handed down as dispensations from on high. And it is an invitation to recalibrate identitarian borders that were porous only from Europe to the rest of the world rather than vice versa. By accepting a representational stratagem in which physicality equals identity, we only further a colonial mind-set that insisted on such an equation. It is in the colonial mind-set, after all, that identity is transformed from effect to cause and anchored in bodily legibility.

Shonibare's art tries to force a wedge between the body and identity by focusing on the travails of desire. Little wonder, then, that he is not considered "African enough." His art uncovers the hybrid transnational history of the "authentically" African while also using it to clothe headless dandies who are themselves unreadable sexually and culturally. These mannequins complicate the ways in which we think of identity and desire by interrupting the straight line between bodies and identities; they ask us to introduce into the colonial equation of physique and ontology a detour that takes note also of desires that cannot be recognized visually alone. Rather than thinking of the critique of Shonibare, then—as the syntax of not "African enough" suggests—in terms of lack, it is more compelling to speak about his art as marking an excess (Shonibare's term) and a superabundance (Badiou's term). For Shonibare, "[E]xcess is the only legitimate means of subversion . . . a form of disobedience, a parasitic disobedience on the host of the species, an excessive form of libido . . . joyful sex."⁹ Insisting on the endless readability of bodies, Shonibare's excess is the artistic equivalent of Freud's overdetermination, where the more readings there are, the less fixed is the meaning. The Dutch Wax figures give rise to a plethora of possibilities that militates against a singular causal identity predicated on bodily difference. This endless readability opens us up to the bewildering realm of indifference that, for all its bewilderment, is the realm in which we live our daily lives.

More rather than less, excess rather than lack: this is the mantra by which Shonibare's art lives. His incredibly detailed installations, intricately tailored clothes, the gorgeous sets that form the backdrop for his photos—all these are instantiations of the excessiveness of Shonibare's travels. This "excess" refers not to the physical props alone but also to the presence of desire in what could—and many would prefer it if it did—have been a straightforward presentation of colonial inequity. Shonibare's art has threads that do not need to be there; ruffs that do not belong. It is precisely this sense of being unnecessary, wasteful, decadent, that forms the stuff of Shonibarean excess, that refuses to allow us to understand with finality precisely by giving us too much to read.

Indeed, despite a colonial insistence on the readability of "native" bodies by skin color and clothing, our dress often refuses to provide redress to the fantasy of colonial legibility. The vestiges of this colonial fantasy, though, continue to haunt us. People from formerly colonized countries consider it a mark of upward mobility to wear "Western" clothes like jeans and T-shirts. But most Westerners have felt wary, in the name of cultural sensitivity, of reciprocally wearing African or Indian clothes; indeed, the ones who have done so have been pilloried for their colonial mind-set. Counterintuitively, Shonibare's experiments with cloth suggest that *not* wearing African or Asian clothes pays obeisance to borders that may have marked the end of colonization but only furthered the intransigence of identity as a colonial legacy. What would a world look like in which a hijab is not automatically seen as non-Western, and bright colors not immediately ascribed an Eastern provenance? Despite living in a so-called globalized world, in which cotton from Mexico might be spun in Bangladesh, stitched in India, tailored in China, warehoused in Brazil, and worn in London, we continue to think that each of these countries has its own specific identity that cannot be disturbed. Traversing differences seems to have—ironically, impossibly—entrenched us in them even more deeply.

Which is to say that the creation of borders is more often than not a motivated act that supports global capitalism despite capitalism's avowed practice of working across borders. Such creations then further impel the managerial impulse to control the difference one has delineated. This is the thrust of the famous and seemingly cosmopolitan HSBC advertisements on television and at international airports.[10] Announcing itself as "The World's Local Bank," HSBC runs a series of ads that take the "same" product or image and assigns different values to them depending on different local contexts. So a square of chocolate is described as "energy," "indulgence," or "sex." And a carpet is described as "décor," "souvenir," and "place of prayer." The tagline on these hoardings notes: "The more you look at the world the more you recognise how people value things differently." On the television ads, the tagline states: "At HSBC we never underestimate the importance of local knowledge." In every case, we are invited to think of the "same" thing as being different from itself, which is a wonderful idea for a bank to contemplate. But then we notice that this "difference" is valued only because it can be managed (by HSBC). Difference becomes a tool by which to judge performance—the bank that is the best at managing difference wins the differences sweepstakes. And as long as there is a universal currency converter in which one can exchange difference, profits can be made anywhere in the world. Far from providing for an anti-ontology, such an investment in difference mandates ontology in order to maximize profits from seemingly absolute differences. Invested as it is in keeping difference intact in order to sell itself as the necessary negotiator among those differences, HSBC both creates and reifies difference. Its flag flies over a boat of difference that sails to their sales rather than across the seven seas.

Clearly, difference is profitable, and not only economically so. Politically, there is much to be gained from proclaiming an ideological respect for difference even in the face of scant regard for differences. Consider, for instance, as Badiou does, the anodyne liberalism that righteously intones the political value of a difference that it cannot itself allow:

That there are intertwined histories, different cultures, and more generally, differences already abundant in one and the "same" individual, that the world is multicolored, that one must let people live, eat, dress, imagine, love in whichever way they please, is not the issue, whatever certain disingenuous simpletons may want us to think. Such liberal truisms are cheap, and one would only like to see those who proclaim them not react so violently whenever confronted with the slightest serious attempt to dissent from their own puny liberal difference. Contemporary cosmopolitanism is a beneficent reality. We simply ask that its partisans not get themselves worked up at the sight of a young veiled woman, lest we begin to fear that what they really desire, far from a web of shifting differences, is the uniform dictatorship of what they take to be "modernity."[11]

With brutal brilliance, Badiou bares the hypocrisy at the heart of a liberalism that preaches the cult of accepting difference yet balks at living with differences. (The Netherlands, which insists that new immigrants not blanch at images of homosexuality put up at immigration checks, nonetheless feels free to ban the burkha; a case in point of a society choosing which version of difference passes muster and which does not.) The dictatorship of uniformity that demands, in effect, that everyone be Western, modern, and rational harks back to an Enlightenment universalism that often insisted on the wholeness of the rational man. In its current avatar, such a universalism is presented as enlightened democratic socialism; everyone still has to look the same, but that sameness is now framed as equality. Shonibare's installations, by contrast, are queer inasmuch as they insist on a universe and a universalism that is fractured, incomplete, surprising. It is the fracture that is universal, not a fantasmatic wholeness that would in effect abolish differences by enshrining them in their fixed places.

For Shonibare, what fractures wholeness is desire. Desires of the body, for the body, and on the body, are representational registers to which Shonibare keeps returning in his art. Resistant as he is to bodily legibility, Shonibare's bodies never have heads, and those that do have helmets over their heads with black paint beneath the surface so we cannot see their faces. In a world in which the phobia about the veiled Muslim woman, for instance, bases itself on the "indecency" of not being able to see her face, Shonibare's faceless sculptures challenge us to rethink our obsession with bodies in general, and faces in particular, as locators of desire and anchors of identity. The faceless mannequins throw light on what Badiou describes as the pieties of first-world democracy; rather than giving us an easy basis for identity, Shonibare makes us travel endlessly in search of it. And at the end of that travail, we find that difference does not ground ontology and ontology can never equal the body.

Indeed, in their resistance to national, racial, and sartorial identity, Shonibare's sculptures shun specificity while theorizing a queer universalism. Not only do they endlessly cross national boundaries, but they are also dandies who are excessive and therefore difficult to read sexually. One might even refer to them as transsexual—in the etymological sense of going beyond sexual identity—and transnational—again in the etymological sense of crossing geopolitical boundaries of nation-states as Marx's workers do. Shonibare's art insists on interruption, and not as an abstract ideal. Instead, by shredding the link between fabric and person, Shonibare asks us to think of the reality in which people live rather than the convenient categories into which we want to slot them. Such a reality takes on board the possibility that a black man can migrate to London from Nigeria and think of himself as English, or that a white person can move from Canada to Kenya and think of herself as Kenyan. Even as Shonibare's art refuses identificatory categories, it maintains an active engagement with the dynamics of how we live and the distances that bodies travel. If we are indeed interested in difference, we must learn to allow its existence instead of demanding that it speak the language understood by the majority. Shonibare's language is a deliberately minoritarian language, one that does not subscribe to the majoritarian protocols of identity.

This understanding of minoritarianism is conceptual rather than numerical—it is what Deleuze and Guattari identify as the opposite of "becoming-fascist."[12] Adopting a minoritarian stance involves looking at issues—including and especially the issue of difference—differently from how we commonly perceive them. Shonibare's minoritarian discourse is an obstacle to the status quo because it removes ontology as the basis for how we live and does not offer to replace it with anything else. Indeed, substituting one content with another does not make a dent in *the way in which* we think, perceive, and analyze the world. Thus, *replacing* sexuality with a different marker of bodily identity—ethnic or gendered or racial—does not change the way in which we read bodies and ascribe ontological essence to them. Instead of only adding new content with which to flesh out his art, Shonibare, who often redoes the "Masters" like Fragonard and Goya, introduces one new element that forces us to reevaluate the regime by which we think we know. For instance, in a series of photographs on the deaths of famous artists, Shonibare sometimes introduces a black character—as a doctor, a lover, a maid. Leonardo da Vinci dies in the arms of Francis I, played by a black man with lustrous curls. Whether or not this is historically "true," such an insertion ensures that we look again. And when we look again, what we see does not match up to what we expect to see—Leonardo with a black lover, and equally, a black man who is not dressed differently from anyone around him and at whose presence no one seems aghast. The introduction of black people into the picture certainly addresses the postcolonial insistence on representational redressal. But the introduction of black people into the picture also asks us to be *indifferent* to that representation because such indifference is the only form of redressal with any political value. By dislocating the settings in which we imagine black and white people, these photographs also unsettle who we imagine black and white people to be. If the photo had given us a "black Leonardo," then it would simply have been a photo negative of a white Leonardo. But by giving us an indifferent smattering of black and white people, this color photograph confuses the norm instead of simply reversing it. It challenges *how* we look rather than catering simply to what we see.

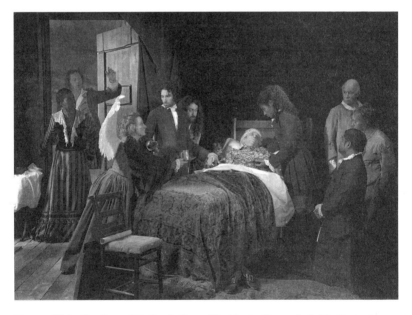

Figure 4. Yinka Shonibare, *Fake Death Picture (The Death of Leonardo da Vinci in the Arms of Francis I—Francois-Guillaume Ménageot)*, 2011. Copyright Yinka Shonibare. Courtesy the artist, Stephen Friedman Gallery, London and James Cohan Gallery, New York

Shonibare's political and artistic engagement necessitates confuting the one-to-one relation between bodies and identities that we are increasingly urged to take for granted in matters of both race and sexuality. In order to move away from this demand for the identitarian specificity of bodies, Shonibare removes the faces from his mannequins. The artist has said he wants his sculptures to elude easy racial identification; in some sculptures, this desire for difficulty is matched also with neutral skin tones on the mannequins—neither black nor white nor brown, the mannequins are instead a sort of beige, which is in any case insignificant beneath the riot of colors that make up the Dutch Wax fabric with which Shonibare clothes them. When they do have faces, it is often not a human face at all, thus making the search for an ontological particular very difficult indeed. *Revolution Kid (Fox)* from 2012 has the face of a fox and the body of a man, *Revolution Kid (Calf)* has the head of a calf, *Planets in my Head, Philosophy* (2011) has a planet for a head, while *Water* (2010) has a water faucet for a head and the body has a hand holding a goblet into which the water falls. So no head or face in the conventional, human, sense, but an eruption of something other in the place we look to for the self. In addition to providing no (recognizable) face, Shonibare also clothes his mannequins fully, giving us no room in which to peep at the body except perhaps for the hands. Though bodies dominate Shonibare's representational landscape, he does not give them to us on a platter. Or rather, he puts them on a platter and thereby does not give them to us; instead, he calls into question the easy equation with which we arrive at a notion of "the human." Fully covered bodies and no distinct faces: What identitarian ontology do these support?

Unless we are indifferent to particularity, our politics will only ever succeed in passing on the content of oppression onto other groups. Politics in any one particular name is not a politics that opens the doors to difference; it rather creates doors that can be banged shut in the face of those still clamoring to get in from the outside. Indeed, we lose out on the queer edge of politics by giving it a local habitation and a name. This is the entire dilemma of multiculturalism: to specify that some cultures are different is also to point out that they are different from the norm; in so doing, one ends up upholding the norm every bit as fully as one might have wanted to oppose it. Naming a culture as such is also to fix the boundaries around it. These differentiated cultures are then brought together as multiple, but they remain in reality a collection of particulars that are rewarded and punished for being separately knowable. This process of

Figure 5. Yinka Shonibare, *Revolution Kid (Fox)*, 2012. Copyright Yinka Shonibare. Courtesy of the artist and Museum Beelden aan Zee, The Hague

knowledge formation is what Foucault has identified as the working of power. Indeed, power flourishes most via its injunction that we speak the "truth" about ourselves and our identities.[13] Even as it pretends to spread respect and human rights universally, it categorizes and polices those rights most effectively. If speaking the language of the law is the only way of being recognized by the law, then inclusion in state-sanctioned modes of cultural and sexual specificity also indicates immediate co-optation by the state's categories of identity.

A liberal politics would advocate for just such inclusion to fight the system from within itself. But a radical politics would ask us to be suspicious of these categories altogether because they both assume and create a chain of expectations that are violent, to say the least. Whether it is the category of race or the category of sexuality, they assume certain truths about the body, and then translate those truths into behavioral truisms. This does not mean that we remain blind to differences among peoples and cultures and colors and sexualities and identities—as if that were even possible. But it does mean that we interrupt the chain of causality that all these categories imply in their formulation. Being indifferent to cultural and sexual specificity means not acquiescing to the state's formulation of categories of knowledge. These categories generate a contest for belonging that is premised on creating demographics of not belonging. Naming creates conditions of scarcity because only so many people can be called by the same name. And when narrative, social, and economic resources ride on definitive answers, they give rise to phobic questions: Is homosexuality African? Is gayness a white person's disease? Can you be gay if you do not have sex? Can you be white if one of your parents is black?

Indifference to categories of identity cannot be recuperated in the service of an anodyne desire for "choice." Indeed, if we change the location of our thinking from identity to universalism, then we short-circuit the causal chain linking skin color or sexual acts to identity. Far from suggesting that we-can-be-whoever-we-want-to-be, this interruption does not allow us the positive (Hegelian) knowledge that a liberal humanism would like us to possess. Instead, it empties out content from these categories so that we can endlessly be surprised by ourselves and others. Sexual acts and skin color would no longer provide a shortcut for a person's intellect, emotions, and politics. We would have to do things the hard way and actually reconceptualize how to traverse differences without designating them as identitarian particulars.

Indeed, the shortcut to conceptualization is precisely what Shonibare and his art militate against. "At a gallery talk in London, a young Black British woman asked [Shonibare] if he had a problem with being black. He replied that he didn't have a problem with being black, but he did have a problem with other people's ideas of what being black should mean for his work."[14] The causal connection between blackness and politics attempts to reinstate a biological basis for the universe. And while it may praise itself for associating blackness with a "radical" politics, that association is as conservative as the one that links blackness with a regressive politics. In a classic production of such a politics, a Marxist critic cites Shonibare's irreverent attitude to identity only to dismiss it for being insufficiently political. In particular, she takes exception to an interview in which Shonibare says: "Wouldn't it be good to just surprise people: Black people can laugh, too! We're not serious all the time! I felt that it was time to loosen up a little. When I make work I draw from my own experiences. But my experiences are not all gloomy."[15] The critic's response to this quotation is to tell us to read Shonibare "against the grain"[16] because "the work of imagining alternatives to capitalism is ... hampered when potentially devastating critiques (such as Shonibare's installations) are tamed by reinscription into more palatable narratives, [when] identity crisis displaces domination and the endless play of signifiers elbows exploitation from view."[17]

Exploitation can and does exist on several different levels, and the critic is quite right in calling attention to its ubiquitous nature. But assuming the fixed identity of the body is itself exploitative to a high degree—this is the one idea that has united theorists from Foucault to Badiou. Not taking seriously the complication of identity is exploitative precisely because it assumes that bodies *should be* legible in similar ways. Not only does such a belief destroy any lingering remnants of difference by placing the same demand on *every* body, but it also presumes to script the language that *should be* spoken by each of these bodies. The irony of this belief in bodily legibility is overwhelming because each type of body is only allowed to speak one language: the body can act as the guarantor only of *certain* truths. Whatever does not fit into a particular political script in this monolingual universe is then dismissed as irrelevant or even dangerous. And so Yinka Shonibare's blackness is meant to connote in only one way, and when it does not, he is accused of not being "African enough."

What might it mean for us to be *indifferent* to Shonibare's blackness in the same way that his sculptures are indifferent to sexual and racial identity?

Clearly, for centuries colonial powers were callously indifferent to the plight of their colonies, a legacy that continues to haunt us even today. But callousness is not the same thing as indifference; indeed, one might argue that callousness is undergirded by a very real if phobic regard for the other, where the difference of the other fills the mind's canvas to such an extent that the consequence is a brutally paranoid empire. Unlike indifference, callousness insists on knowable ethnic and sexual difference. Such specificity was responsible for colonialism, and it is a matter of no small irony that it also forms the backbone of a multiculturalism in which the bantustans of specificity follow the logic of colonial endeavors. Ascribing a bodily basis for identity and then generating laws to govern that base returns us to the logic of colonialism with its insistence on biological difference and identitarian immobility. Shonibare's art complicates that causal chain to expose us to an indifferent universe in which there is no necessary correlation between how one looks and what one does. Sculptures without faces recall the specter of the veiled Muslim woman whose unseen face causes much consternation—on the left because covering her face is allegedly a denial of her individuality, and on the right because not being able to see her face deters the checking of terrorism. In Shonibare's world, a woman with a hijab may not even be a Muslim, and even if she were, wearing a hijab would not be a ticket to her being in the world; the correlation between hijab and "backwardness" that has prompted so much phobic European legislation would simply not exist if we were to think indifferently about identity.

Cornelia Klinger has noted that "at no point did identity 'become' a problem; it was a 'problem' from its birth ... [and] could exist only as a problem. ... 'Identity' is a name given to the escape sought from uncertainty."[18] What would it mean *not* to escape from uncertainty, not to give in to identitarian causality? This question does not seek to minimize the fact that we all have bodies and identities to which we are deeply attached and that we dearly cherish. It tries, rather, to resuscitate the most commonplace experience that has somehow become lost in the rush to identity politics: that we are never fully any one or multiple things. We are always moving across and beyond markers attributed to us. Universalism asks us to consider this impossibility of identity seriously because it is the condition of the real world in which genetic, linguistic, regional, and sexual purity barely and rarely exists. The pleasure of universalism is the pleasure of what seems impossible but is ubiquitously present. Indeed, when Anthony

Figure 6. Yinka Shonibare, *Headless Man Trying to Drink*, 2005. Courtesy of the artist and Collection of Melva Bucksbaum and Raymond Learsy

Downey noted in an interview with Yinka Shonibare that he "was . . . intrigued by the impossibility of it all . . . : the impossibility of headless people having sex, for example, or the impossibility of eighteenth-century costumes made of African fabric" or of headless people bending over a water fountain, Shonibare replied: "I enjoy presenting 'impossibility.'"[19] *Soyons réalistes, demandons l'impossible!*—let us be realistic, let us demand the impossible!—is the cry of revolution that Shonibare has adopted from the French ferment of 1968.

As Badiou describes it, this impossible enjoyment, this impossible desire, is the "multiplicity that, exceeding itself, upholds universality. Its being in excess of itself precludes its being represented as a totality. Super-abundance cannot be assigned to any Whole. That is precisely why it legitimates the destitution of difference."[20] Shonibare's African-print fabric similarly "assumes a chameleon-like role since it can be viewed, depending on one's perspective, as African, European, colonial, imperialist, and even global. . . . In Shonibare's art, the polarities of signs referring to colonizing powers, as well as colonised and post-colonised peoples, are undermined by the excess of their costumes and gestures that . . . partially eradicates the firmly held political positions of any one group."[21] His sculptures do not lend themselves to being African or gay even as they deal with colonialism and desire. Rather, they are deeply skeptical of the regime of power/knowledge in which the body is expected to speak certain truths that then become its identity.

Universalism allows us instead never to feel quite at home in our "own" skin and in our "own" countries. It encourages us to be xenophiles who enjoy the superabundance of our desires without prescribing a fixed identity for them. It allows us to embrace our identities in the indifferent knowledge that we have several more up our sleeve. It urges us to renegotiate the ways in which we think and look. And it allows us to be homosexuals or blacks without tying down those descriptors to the body in one direction, and ontology in the other. Indeed, queer universalism, as the art of enjoying the impossible, and being militantly loyal to it, urges us to be indifferent to sexual and ethnic particularity. Alain Badiou and Yinka Shonibare are joined in this enjoyment by William Shakespeare's Antony, whose love for the Egyptian queen in *Antony and Cleopatra* is described as "o'erflow[ing] the measure" (1.1.2), and who insists that "[t]here's beggary in the love that can be reckon'd" (1.1.15).

CURATING DESIRE

I will turn again to Shakespeare in the next chapter, but for now I want to explore the very idea of the museum as a space, not of confinement, but of errancy. The museum that showcased both Yinka Shonibare MBE's art and ethnicity might have been chosen, I suggested earlier, because there is as yet no Museum of Desire in the world. But soon I discovered just such a museum. The only difference is that instead of being a building made of wood or brick and mortar, this one is the title of an unpublished short story by John Berger.

"The Museum of Desire"—both the story and the building described in the story—is set in an eighteenth-century house, "built just before the French Revolution," that has recently been turned into a museum showcasing the many splendors acquired by its owners.[22] Like Shonibare, who too favors the eighteenth century as the setting for his fashion sensibility, Berger's museum contains several relics from the Napoleon and Josephine–Louis XV and Madame de Pompadour days that evoke the guillotined heads of Shonibare's mannequins. Shonibare's headless mannequins literally decapitate the Enlightenment discourse of universal reason; Berger's museum replaces the seeming seamlessness of universal reason with the universal interruptions of desire. The museum has many objects of desire, organized sometimes according to national boundaries—"the Dutch section"—but sometimes seemingly at random: "Many of the paintings on display feature young women and shot game, both subjects testifying to the pursuit of passion." The narrator of the story, taken with the striking voice and appearance of a docent dressed in black, joins a group on a tour of the museum collections.[23] What follows is a story that is part straightforward narrative about the treasures in the museum and their historical significance, part archive of feelings as the narrator encounters various artifacts of beauty, part art catalogue-cum-gossip rag about artists' lives and their subjects, and part magical realist tale as the narrator enters the space of the plastic bag being carried by the docent as she leaves the museum after a day's work. Contained in that bag are nine presents, all wrapped and some addressed, all to and for an unknown person. The narrator describes all nine presents, sometimes inserting himself into the aura evoked by a particular present, and then the story ends.

This multitude of presents seems to address specific demands that friends/lovers/colleagues might have made over time on the docent of the museum. However, at the same time as each present appears to be small and specific, it is also enigmatic, and the line of connection among them is unclear. In their simultaneous specificity and nonspecificity, the motley collection of wrapped gifts seems to address the very difference *(spaltung)* that Jacques Lacan theorizes between demand and desire. For him, demand appears to coalesce around a specific need, but supplying that need makes clear that demand exceeds its specific fulfillment; this remainder of demand gets expressed as a desire that can never be filled: "Demand in itself bears on something other than the satisfaction it calls for. It is demand for a presence or an absence.... Demand already constitutes the Other as having the 'privilege' of satisfying needs, that is, the power to deprive them of what alone can satisfy them. The Other's privilege here thus outlines the radical form of the gift of what the Other does not have—namely . . . its love" (579–80).[24]

After it lists the many gifts designed to meet demand and fall short of desire, the story suddenly ends. The ending is abrupt—for a long time I searched in vain for the "full" story—and the story as it stands does not tell us anything about anything. Who is the docent? Why is the narrator fascinated by her? For whom is she taking the presents, and why did she lug them all the way to work? Are these presents to give away, or has she just received them? If the latter, then why is the note in her handwriting? What does the inscription on the note—"When a man is loved he leaves the chorus like long ago and becomes a king"—mean, and why does it use the American teenage slang of "like"? What is the relationship between narrator and narrated? Who owned what has now become the museum and how did they collect all these objects? Is the actual museum called The Museum of Desire, or is that simply the title of the short story? The story tells us nothing at all except that it is a story about desire. And here are some of the things it says about desire:

> *Desire is a trick. Desire involves imagination.*
>
> The painted portrait plays a trick, one of the oldest in the world. (Bathsheba was obliged to play it: the trick of appearing to address a stranger, while thinking of somebody else.) For an instant the spectator may suppose that the gestures and smile of the woman in Amsterdam are addressed to him. Yet obviously this is not the case. She was not looking at any spectator. She was looking hard at a man she desired, imagining him as her lover. And this man could only have been Drost. The only thing we know for certain about Drost is that he was desired precisely by this woman.

Desire is fleeting. Desire exceeds meaning.

To be desired is perhaps the closest anybody can reach in this life to feeling immortal. . . . It is hard to describe her face. I studied it again and again and each time, it shifted like a page being turned in a book. Our walk through the galleries began to resemble a walk through a wood. This was a question of how she placed us, herself and what she was talking about. She consistently prevented us from crowding around whatever she was explaining. She pointed out an item as if it were a deer to be glimpsed as it crossed our path between two distant trees. And wherever she directed our attention, she always kept herself elusively to the side, as if she had just stepped out from behind a tree.

Desire is wrapped up. Desire does not reveal its contents.

She was carrying an old flimsy Marks and Spencer's plastic bag which looked as if it might tear, because whatever was in it was too heavy. In the bag were a cauliflower, a pair of resoled shoes and nine wrapped presents. The presents were all for the same person, and each one was numbered and tied up with the same golden twine. In the first was a sea shell, a small conch about the size of a child's fist, perhaps the size of her fist. I was never close enough to really measure. The shell was the color of silver-ish felt, veering toward peach. If one turned it to look inside, the peach was more vivid. The swirls of its brittle encrustations resembled the lace flounces on the dress of the woman on the swing, and its polished interior was as pale as skin habitually sheltered from the sun.

Desire is a heady pleasure. Desire is unreadable.

The fifth present was a paper bag of a brand of sweets called wine gums. This brand has existed for a century. Probably they are the cheapest sweets in the world. Despite their very varied and acid colors, they all taste of pear drops. For me (but they were not for me) no other taste I know evokes so sharply my early childhood. Their flavor remains the flavor of pleasure itself, before I could tie my own shoe laces in double bows. . . .

Her ninth present was a kind of embroidered pin cushion, very small, in the form of a heart. Its stuffing smelled of cinnamon and a perfume I do not know. A note, written in her handwriting, was wrapped around it. It read: "When a man is loved he leaves the chorus like long ago and becomes a king."

Desire is passion. Desire is inappropriate.

"Now we go," she said, holding her head high, "to another part of the wood, the painter has made it morning here, so all is fresh, and everyone is freshly dressed—including the young lady on the swing. No statues of Friendship, all the statues here are Cupids. The swing was put up in the spring. One of her slippers—you notice?—has already been kicked off! Intentionally? Unintentionally? Who can tell? As soon as a young lady, freshly dressed, sits herself there on the seat of the swing, such questions are hard to answer, no feet on the ground. The husband is pushing her from behind. Swing high, swing low. The lover is hidden in the bushes in front of her where she told him to be. Her dress—it's less elaborate, more casual, than Madame de Pompadour's and frankly I prefer it—is of satin with lace flounces. Do you know what they called the red of her dress? They called it peach, though personally I never saw a peach of that color, any more than I ever saw a peach blushing. The stockings are white cotton, a little roughish compared to the skin of the knees they cover. The garters, pink ones to match the slippers, are too small to go higher up the leg without pinching. Notice her hidden lover. The foot, which lost the slipper, is holding up the skirt and petticoats high—their lace and satin rustle softly in the slipstream—and nobody, I promise you, nobody in those days wore underwear! His eyes are popping out of his head. As she intended him to do, he can see all."

The objects in the museum are varied and fabulous. This last description of an object of desire—which appears well before the end of the story—is of Jean-Honoré Fragonard's 1767 painting, *The Swing* (or *The Happy Accidents of the Swing* [*Les hazards heureux de l'escarpolette*]). Presciently anticipating the modern connotations of the happy accidents of "swinging"—a very Lucretian term for sexual licentiousness—the painting depicts a man pushing a swing on which a woman sits with one foot high in the air, and the slipper flying off her foot: her lover is looking at all that is exposed in and by the swinging action. (In Fragonard, the man pushing the swing is possibly the lady's husband, and possibly a priest, thus layering scandal upon scandal.) Seeing Fragonard's swing in "The Museum of Desire" transports us metonymically back to Shonibare, and his 2001 sculpture, *The Swing (after Fragonard)*, in which the flying slipper is high up in the air, and the gaily colored dress frames a black hole where the genitalia is both given to us and withheld from view. We see a knee ringed around by

Figure 7. Jean-Honoré Fragonard, *The Swing*, 1767. By kind permission of the Trustees of the Wallace Collection.

Figure 8. Yinka Shonibare, *The Swing (after Fragonard)*, 2001. Copyright Yinka Shonibare. Courtesy of the artist and Tate Collection, London

a visible garter, and then darkness within (up close one can actually look in to the darkness and see knickers made of the same fabric as the headless mannequin's underskirt). Shonibare's remaking of the Fragonard painting that is now housed in the Wallace Collection in London (thought to be the setting for Berger's short story) allows us a three-dimensional view of the swing of desire, even as the triumvirate of Fragonard–Berger–Shonibare affords us three different pictures of the "same" painting.

The museum of desire is thus a site of excess. We have too many presents, too many sights, too many people, too much stray libido, and too little accountability, too little explanation. Berger's version of the museum features largely European artifacts that are ripe for Shonibare's queer picking; they speak from within borders about desire's universal propensity to stray. Narratives that are in excess of facts, desires that are in excess of bodies, clothes that are in excess of their nationalities, identities that are in excess of their fixings: these are a few of the threads that Shonibare shares in common with his eighteenth- and twentieth-century predecessors. The museums that they imagine and populate cannot contain them even as they are built to house things of specificity. But why museums? How can a museum showcase desire? What do museums have to tell us about desire and indifference and universalism?

These questions are addressed by another artist who has actually built his own museum, though not with the explicit title of desire. Orhan Pamuk's *Museum of Innocence (Masumiyet Müzesi)* appeared as a novel in 2008 and was built as a museum in Istanbul in 2012. Despite or perhaps because of its title, the book and the building read as a museum of desire. In a chapter entitled "The Dogs," the novel speaks about the protagonist Kemal's interest in museums:

> Many years after the events I am relating here, I set out to see all the museums of the world; having spent the day viewing tens of thousands of strange and tiny objects on exhibit in a museum in Peru, India, Germany, Egypt, or any number of other countries, I would down a couple of stiff drinks and spend many hours walking the streets of whatever city I was in. Peering through curtains and open windows in Lima, Calcutta, Hamburg, Cairo, and so many others, I would see families joking and laughing as they watched television and ate the evening meal; I would invent all sorts of excuses to step into these houses, and even to have my picture taken with the occupants. This is how I came to notice that in most of the world's homes there

was a china dog sitting on top of the television set. Why was it that millions
of families all over the world had felt the same need? (513)[25]

The universalism being described here is of a quite literal kind: unlike the
exclusively European provenance of Berger's museum, in this novel people
from around the world, no matter what their nationality—from "any number of other countries"—invest in china dogs as decorations for their television sets; these dogs are universally present, ubiquitous. In itself, this
seems like a fairly innocuous comment. And while it addresses a seeming universality of taste, and insists on an indifference to national boundaries and cultural barriers, it does not really address a universality of desire.
But if we consider that this comment appears in a narrative about doomed
lovers who spend several hundred pages not getting together, then we can
see how the china dogs metonymically suggest something about desire that
Shonibare, too, points to. The china dogs might be named for one country
but are spread all over the world; desire might be housed in one object but
cannot be contained by it. Dogs, like desires, stray.

The novel offers up this stray, restless, wandering desire as an alternative
to what might be termed "monumental" desire, desire that constructs an
explanatory narrative about itself. According to Pamuk, this latter mode is
exemplified by the big museums of the world:

> We are sick and tired of museums that try to construct historical narratives
> of a society, community, team, nation, state, people, company or species. We
> all know that the ordinary, everyday stories of individuals are richer, more
> humane and much more joyful than the stories of colossal cultures.[26]

Although it runs the risk of elevating the individual as the repository of all
that is good and free in the world, Pamuk is critical of the idea that desire
is an individual choice, or that it can be mandated at will. Indeed, his analysis of museums suggests a deep resistance to single narratives; he prefers
instead to focus on singular ones. Thus he notes:

> The museums I visited in my childhood—not just in Istanbul but even
> in Paris, where I first went in 1959—were joyless places infused with the
> atmosphere of a government office. In keeping with their state-sanctioned
> mission, shared by schools, of telling us the "national history" that we were
> supposed to believe in, these large museums held authoritarian displays of

various objects whose purpose we could not quite fathom, belonging to kings, sultans, generals, and religious leaders whose lives and histories were far removed from ours. It was impossible to forge a personal connection with any of the objects displayed in these monumental institutions. Nevertheless, we still knew exactly what we were supposed to feel: respect for that thing known as "national history"; fear of the power of the state; and a humility that overshadowed our own individualities.[27]

This Foucault-like outline of how power works, even and especially through the promotion of high art, is a sobering reminder of how we are all implicated in the project of policing desire and promoting the interests of the state. Power works by pretending that desire can be contained, and every time we get married, for instance, we are extending the illusion through which power reproduces itself. In this way, museums seem, at least intuitively, rather like multiculturalism: they assemble discrete, precisely identified, dead or deadened objects that together form a well-regulated heterogeneous collective; they also privilege certain valued objects over others that are less valued. At the same time, however, museums are also evocative of Lacan's definition of metonymy as "being caught in the rails— eternally stretching forth towards the *desire for something else.*"[28] In museums, the hierarchical synecdoche—that which isolates the part as a representative of an idealized, useful whole—rubs up against an indifferent metonymy, which forges connections with neither propriety nor discretion. Capricious and improper associations push back against motivated extrapolations. In a museum of desire, each term works against the other: the museum wants to collate and order while desire swings metonymically between objects and registers of legibility. Museums of desire are failed enterprises because they cannot forge lasting connections. By focusing on the ubiquitousness of the china dogs, for instance, *The Museum of Innocence* suggests a trajectory for desire that always travels. It can get attached to the thing right next to itself or it can travel a long way before getting hitched or it can roll along without gathering any moss: desire is indifferent in its all-pervasiveness rather than specific in its object-relations. By encasing what *everyone* in the world seems to be doing, the museum paradoxically also encapsulates the impossibility of fixing the world's desire.

The Museum of Innocence, both novel and building, offers us the opposite of monumental history through a single story that is also the story of an entire culture and of several cultures and above all, of desire. A tale of doomed love, at once melodrama and social history, film script and novel, the *Museum* is about the ways in which desire cannot be contained, even and especially in a museum. Kemal and Füsun get together while Kemal is engaged to be married; Kemal goes ahead with his engagement and loses Füsun, it seems, forever. After suffering endless agonies, Kemal breaks off the relationship with his fiancé and insinuates himself into Füsun's family circle, which at this point also includes her husband. There follows eight long years of yearning, sometimes agonized and often enjoyable, filled with little acts of kleptomania in which Kemal secrets away objects that belong to Füsun or that she might have touched. Despite being a museum, then, what *Masumiyet Müsezi* does is to showcase the metonymic slide of desire, where every one of the 4,213 cigarette butts that Kemal collects both depict and fail to contain Füsun. The museum has eighty-three glass cases to match the novel's eighty-three chapters; each case bears the chapter heading from the book, and the objects on display are stunning in their simultaneous lucidity and opacity.

One such chapter/vitrine heading is "A Few Unpalatable Anthropological Truths." The chapter in the novel describes the sexual plight of women in 1970s Turkey, while the museum display features prominently the following photograph meant to correspond to this paragraph from the novel:

> If the man tried to wriggle out of marrying the girl, and the girl in question was under eighteen years of age, an angry father might take the philanderer to court to force him to marry her. Some such cases would attract press attention, and in those days it was the custom for newspapers to run the photographs with black bands over the "violated" girls' eyes, to spare their being identified in this shameful situation. Because the press used the same device in photographs of adulteresses, rape victims, and prostitutes, there were so many pictures of women with black bands over their eyes that to read a Turkish newspaper in those days was like wandering through a masquerade. All in all, Turkish newspapers ran very few photographs of Turkish women without bands over their eyes. (83–84)[29]

These pictures are clearly photographs rather than newspaper clippings, and the black bands have been superimposed upon them in exactly the same manner as the protagonist describes the Turkish press as having done. Pamuk illustrates what the newspapers intended to demonstrate:

that the shame of desire leads to a loss of identity. This loss of identity is instituted in the name of protecting the women from further ignominy, but the effect is to establish a causal relation between the malpractices attendant on desire and a loss of self. In a very different way from Shonibare, then, Pamuk too shows us how desire is bound up with loss rather than reinforcement. The main narrative of the novel is all about that loss and the lengths to which we go to guard against it. Interestingly, whenever Pamuk has had to defend in interviews his protagonist against charges of obsessiveness, he claims Kemal is Everyman, that his love for Füsun— described in reviews as obsessive, neurotic, frightening, wasteful—is ours.

Pamuk is critical of desire being described in terms of shame as it is in the Turkish newspapers of which he writes. For him, desire exists as a superabundance, indifferent to differences of person and climate, that can fill a 728-page novel. Just as Kemal's desire cannot be anchored, so too the novel spills over into the museum and vice versa; indeed, there is now also a catalogue to accompany the museum called *The Innocence of Objects*. This continual spillage of desire echoes Slavoj Žižek's comment on Badiou's notion of the event: "[A]ll of the multitude of Being cannot ever be adequately represented in a State of Being, and an Event always occurs at the site of this surplus/remainder which eludes the grasp of the State."[30] If we are tempted to hope that all would have been well *if only* Kemal had honored his initial attraction to Füsun, then we are not good readers of a desire that cannot be contained by the differentiating institutions sanctioned by the state. This renegade desire runs throughout the novel, and the novel's conclusion reinforces the link between desire and tragedy. Kemal's dying statement about himself at the very end only repeats this link in an ironic register: "Let everyone know, I lived a very happy life" (728).

This life, filled with loss, sorrow, and objects, always objects, is a life of desire. Perhaps for Kemal it really was happy. Most people fetishize the teleology of desire, its fulfillment in the object of one's desire; but for Kemal and Füsun, that fulfillment is not the thing in which happiness lies. In fact, the novel actively, repeatedly, and determinedly refuses fulfillment. Instead, Pamuk's masked ladies mirror Shonibare's headless mannequins in highlighting the devastating disruptions of desire. For Kemal, these devastations are the stuff of happiness, a oneness with a world in which everyone suffers the same pangs of love, though most choose not to recognize them. By focusing on objects, Kemal invites us to indulge in the fantasy that things do indeed fulfill desire. But by giving us a continual metonymic

Figure 9. This image from the Museum of Innocence in Istanbul corresponds to the chapter "A Few Unpalatable Anthropological Truths" from the novel. Copyright of the Innocence Foundation and Refik Anadol

slide of objects—indeed, by overwhelming us with, for instance, 4,213 cigarette butts smoked by Füsun—Pamuk shows up the inadequacy of any object to fulfill desire. The "attachment to objects" that Pamuk says is what everyone develops after facing a trauma in love is shown to be as traumatic as the cause that occasioned it: it is the trauma of coming face-to-face with the superabundance of desire.[31]

Desire thrives on not being fulfilled: in the novel as in life, this is what makes it sexy. Objects cannot contain desire, no matter how many of them one crams into a museum. Difference does not account for desire because desire is universally abundant. Such are the treasures contained in a museum of desire.

2 Disembodying the Cause

Shakespeare's Dramatic Elisions

What if "the negative where all identity is lost, starting with the very identity of the body writing," far from being a denial of the body, is actually the body's own denial of the category of identity? What if sexuality were not a type of identity but a type of loss of identity?

—Barbara Johnson, "Bringing out D. A. Miller"

For Shonibare, desire is that which does not subscribe to a relation of cause and effect. Bodies cannot explain desire, and objects cannot contain it. Race cannot ground the self, and exhibitions make it travel. Difference cannot sustain it, and queerness haunts it at every step. If we press further on this strange but rich nexus of performance-bodies-desire-ontology-queerness, then the next question to consider is how desire can be recognized in a performing and performed body, in a social body that stages itself self-consciously. Yinka Shonibare MBE has already suggested some answers for staged figures, but for bodies in motion we need to look to the stage. How do we read a body on stage and apprehend its desire? There are of course some obvious signs: swooning lovers swearing undying love to one another. Blazons of a lover's attributes. Jealous plots to frame ex-lovers or retrieve old flames. Statues that move. Characters who freeze. Lines that exalt. Rhetoric that sweeps lovers off their feet. In the theater, all these markers of desire depend on a body to deliver lines or be the recipient of them; to be bruised or praised; to swoon or soar. But how do we see desire on stage in the absence of a body? Can desire be present without a physicality to guarantee its presence? If Shonibare removes the face in order to force attention on a colorfully clothed body, then what happens if that body too is removed? The problem is a peculiarly theatrical one, since the theater is the only literary arena that calls for physical bodies to enact its tales; it is also a pressingly social one since what bodies *do* forms the basis of what we desire to do with them. Is desire always based in a material substrate or does theater allow us to theorize a *nonmaterial desire*—desire without a body—that would flesh out Shonibare's use of headless mannequins?

Just as Shonibare speaks about the unreadability of bodies clothed in gorgeous materials, William Shakespeare theorizes the nonmateriality of bodies in relation to desire. *A Midsummer Night's Dream*, for instance, asks us to think about what happens to desire in the absence of a body. At first, this appears to be a peculiar question to be posed by this particular play. After all, there is no dearth of bodies in this text; if anything, there is an excess. The play requires so many actors that theatrical productions since Peter Brook's Royal Shakespeare Company performance in 1970 have taken to doubling the roles of Hippolyta/Theseus and Titania/Oberon. In addition to the several bodies on stage, the play also frequently discourses on bodies and their relation to desire. Take, for instance, Theseus's famous speech on the imagination in act 5 of the play, in which he dismisses the lovers' story about their night spent together in the forest:[1]

> *Theseus*: . . . . The lover, all as frantic,
> Sees Helen's beauty in a brow of Egypt.
> . . . .
> And as imagination bodies forth
> The forms of things unknown, the poet's pen
> Turns them to shapes, and gives to airy nothing
> A local habitation and a name.
> Such tricks hath strong imagination
> That if it would but apprehend some joy
> It comprehends some bringer of that joy;
> Or in the night, imagining some fear,
> How easy is a bush supposed a bear! (5.1.10–11, 14–22)[2]

In an argument the play explores more fully, Theseus suggests that in order to make fantasies real, people inevitably locate desire in a body. The body is concretized by the desiring imagination and is thus only a fantasmatic entity. Hippolyta adds, a moment later:

> But all the story of the night told over,
> And all their minds transfigured so together,
> More witnesseth than fancy's images,
> And grows to something of great constancy;
> But howsoever, strange and admirable. (5.1.23–27)

Though they are both talking about imaginative desire and its relation to truth, Theseus and Hippolyta fundamentally disagree with each other, as the very first word of Hippolyta's response—"But"—makes clear. For her, the ability to make concrete is the reason one should heed the imagination, while for Theseus it is the reason to mistrust it. Hippolyta is convinced that the imagination bestows more credibility on its narratives, not less, but for Theseus, conjuring a coherent entity in which desire can anchor itself is mere fantasy. The imagination, for Hippolyta, is far greater than the sum of its parts—the lovers' stories together testify to the "constancy" of love—but for Theseus, this alignment among their stories only betrays the extent of their fevered imagination. According to him, the "bodies" that imagination brings forth are shapes intended to create a causal link between a bringer of joy and the joy itself, where no such link exists. Imagination thus sets up a direct correspondence between happiness–bliss–joy, on the one hand, and a body responsible for producing those feelings, on the other. This correspondence is, more forcefully for Theseus than for Hippolyta, *imaginary*. In a play in which the production and identification and transformation of bodies is crucial to both plot and rhetoric, Theseus's argument about the fantasmatic bodily materialization of an imaginative desire invites us to consider its inverse correlate: the possibility of a non-material desire that is not necessarily located in a physical body.

Theseus uses the word "joy," which of course is not desire; in fact joy is often regarded as the opposite of desire. But the psychoanalytic term *jouissance*, which describes both pain and joy, forges a link between joy and desire in which the latter tempers the merely happy associations of the former. Untranslatable as either the one or the other, much like Theseus's speech, *jouissance* is often rendered as joy, but it is also the sundering of that joy, the moment at which one gets a glimpse of nonbeing and non-meaning. Describing it in Lacanian terms as the "unnameable" remainder of the Real in the Symbolic, Lee Edelman argues that "jouissance, sometimes translated as 'enjoyment,'" is "a movement beyond the pleasure principle, beyond the distinction of pleasure and pain, a violent passage beyond the bounds of identity, meaning, and law. This passage . . . may have the effect, insofar as it gets attached to a particular object or end, of congealing identity around the fantasy of satisfaction or fulfillment by means of that object" (25).[3] In Lacanian terms, the embodied "joy" of which Theseus speaks is the congealed object of desire, a fantasmatic solidity conjured up to tie down the "unknown[ness]" of desire.

Might we name this congealed solidity the body? As a single name given to a collection of limbs and feelings, the body stands in a privileged relation to the self. Despite being dismissed by Descartes as the unreliable barometer of the mind's truth, bodies have always been around in our theoretical idiolects, especially in conversations around multiculturalism, race and sexuality studies, and even performance studies. Theories from performativity to posthumanism have fiercely attempted to nuance an investment in the transparency of bodies but have succeeded only to varying degrees. No matter how many its acknowledged peculiarities and inconsistencies, state and academic cultures seem invested in understanding "the body" as superimposing a regime of singular legibility.[4] In the case of desire, the status of the body is widely considered the paramount marker of identity—what a body *is* explains its desire, and then our desire for it. So what do we do with a body in *A Midsummer Night's Dream* in relation to which much desire is generated, but which is imaginary to the extent that it does not exist in the text *as* a body? A body that does not "grow to something of great constancy," "howsoever strange and admirable" its trace in the play? I am speaking about the Indian boy, the subject of Oberon and Titania's quarrel, who never appears in a speaking or nonspeaking part in the text as written but who occupies significant time in the play as the subject of much conversation, frequently invoked as the cause of Titania and Oberon's estrangement from one another.[5]

The boy's present yet nonmaterialized body performs a crucial theatrical function. From the point of view of the text, *none* of the characters has a body: they are all imaginary and implied, except insofar as the language designates physical features or an actual presence. The boy's physical absence from the play-text thus makes even more visible the fictive and "imaginary" (in Theseus's sense) condition of the body itself. Contrary to what we often believe, characters do not actually exist on stage in bodily form—the actor's body simply takes on the character, and the boy's absent body here makes this imaginary condition of all bodies in the play-text especially evident. But despite not having a body—or having only an imaginary one—the boy performatively occupies significant time on both page and stage.

Generations of directors have solved this puzzle of immateriality by materializing the absent body and creating the Indian boy as a character on stage and on screen. The boy is never given any words, of course, but he is inevitably presented as beautiful, desirable, and mysteriously exotic. Scholars of race and colonialism have critiqued this representation as being imperialistic for reducing the Indian boy to an exotic spectacle.[6] While this may be true of certain productions, what is even more interesting is that the absence of the Indian boy from the text, the inability to conjure him from airy nothingness, creates an anxiety among textual interpreters that assuages itself by insisting on producing an object—the more spectacular the better. To ensure that the moving force behind Oberon and Titania's desire does indeed have a body, productions either exoticize the boy— not only does he have a body, but what a body it is!—or infantilize it as if to say, "Pardon the intrusion, but might we suggest the existence at least of a small body, easy to ignore, but nonetheless materially present in its embodiment?" No matter whether he is big or small, fully dressed or naked, the embodied Indian boy is necessarily spectacular because he has nothing to do other than *be*, nothing to offer other than be seen. By frequently exaggerating his physical contours and making him alluring—larger than life and exotic, because that is what they assume desire looks like—productions insist on the boy's bodily presence in order to explain the desire generated by him. The "fault" of such embodiments is not that they might be more or less racist, but that they are all anxious. And far from being a fault, this anxiety rather points to a fault line in notions of desire that the play mines in several different ways.

There are thus two different modes of theatricality operating around the physically absent body of the changeling boy. We might hypothetically attribute the first to "Shakespeare" and the second to "later productions." The first use of theatricality holds the boy "offstage" as always invisible, accentuating the non-self-present nature of all bodies in the play. This mode marks the body as absent—and in doing so marks desire, and the theatricality that stages desire, as nonmaterial. This nonmaterial, absent condition is also nonlogical, noncausal, nonreferential, and nonlocatable. It implies a rupturing of the subject that splits the self from the body, and refuses a clear object for, and cause of, desire. The second use of theatricality tries to foreclose this theoretical insight by bringing some kind of physical body onstage. It tries to assert desire as being physical and material, as referential, as caused and contained and located. The decision about whether or not to physically produce the changeling boy on stage is thus crucial to thinking about the body and its relation to desire.

ABSENT BODY, PRESENT DESIRE

Like Yinka Shonibare's mannequins, Shakespeare's play too questions the imperative to equate particular bodies and desires. While Shonibare speaks in the bloody aftermath of colonial wars waged between racialized bodies, Shakespeare here speaks in the shadow of the spice trade that presaged colonialism. Both the postcolonial Shonibare and the precolonial Shakespeare defy the colonial endeavor of placing boundaries around desire. For the two artists, separated by four hundred years, desire is the thing that eludes the embodying imperative of colonialism; it resists the colonial insistence on fixing identities on the basis of bodily difference. For every desire corralled into policing the boundary between colonial masters and slaves, there are desires that cannot abide by boundaries. Indeed, what is remarkable about this play is not only that there is a changeling Indian boy whom everyone desires and no one sees. What is also remarkable is that no character seems bothered by not seeing him. No one seems concerned that the desired Indian boy does not have a body. What, then, is the relation between the boy's absence and the desire he nonetheless generates?

The Indian boy is introduced to us by Puck when the sprite describes the changeling's role in the fight between his master and mistress. We then see both Oberon and Titania discourse variously about the boy, the one asking for his handover, and the other one refusing it. We even get a lyrical description of his existence *in utero*, when his mother is pregnant with the fetus; but we never get a body. I do not want to speculate on the reasons why Shakespeare withholds the body of the Indian boy from us when he could have been such an interesting character.[7] But I do want to note that from the very beginning of his appearance in the play, the boy is positioned between presence-as-absence (his mother, now dead, then pregnant) and absence-as-presence (himself). Rather than recuperating bodily presence as the essential basis of desire, that without which desire cannot exist, I would like to argue that *A Midsummer Night's Dream*, like Shonibare's art, problematizes the causal link we normally attribute to that relation by giving us a nonmaterial desire that cannot be grounded in a body. If clothes can embody desire but not be reducible to a self, then can desire flourish in the absence of a body?

Despite or because of not having a body, the Indian boy is always positioned in the space and time of desire. This desire attaches to him synecdochally in the mode of nostalgia: the description of his pregnant mother swimming in the perfumed and spicy Indian air; as well as practically: Oberon wants him as his pageboy, Titania wants him in her entourage. The Indian boy is desired, certainly, but in the play this desire also *ensures* his absence, or rather, his absence is the very theme of his desirability. Titania has "stol'n" him from an Indian king, and Oberon in turn steals the boy from Titania. Whether in India or in the woods, with men or women, the boy is repeatedly configured as a thing that is lost, stolen, and even hijacked. Standing at that intersection of an absent presence and a present absence, the Indian boy is always lost from view. He cannot exist except as the backdrop to the drama, even as he is also its ostensible cause. After all, without him, Titania and Oberon would have nothing to quarrel over, the Athenian lovers would go unremarked by Oberon in the forest, Puck would not be sent to get the love potion, Bottom would not be translated into an ass, and the play within the play would not have its audience of multiple newlyweds. Without the Indian boy, the shape of the play (its body?) would have been very different.

Perhaps because of his centrality to the plot, even the earliest recorded production of the play—Henry Purcell's 1692 opera, *The Fairy Queen*—produced the Indian boy as an elaborate part of the play's machinery, as something that makes the play work, and that explains the workings of the play. Without the Indian boy, desire cannot be explained in this play. With him, not only can it be explained, but it can also be staged. The Indian boy allows us to *see* desire and to see it as the condition of sight itself, as the material body without which, supposedly, the play cannot be seen.

Given his importance on both page and stage, then, it is only fitting that we also have a narrative about *why* the boy matters so much to Titania and Oberon. His life has been exchanged for his mother's—we are told that his mother died while giving birth to him—and she was a beloved votaress of Titania's. It is this exchange that gives the boy value for Titania because she wants him as a remembrance of his mother. And it is his value for Titania, we presume, that makes Oberon covet him as his own. Or maybe it is the boy's good looks, his cuteness, that attracts both Titania and Oberon, but this is precisely what we cannot know, since we never *see* the boy in the text and never get a description of him that extends beyond the adjectives "lovely" and "sweet." This sweet and lovely boy, the cause of both discord and concord in the play, of "joy" in both Theseus's and Lacan's sense of the word, does not have a body, yet it is his body that Oberon, Titania, and audiences over the years have insistently wanted.

The doubly absent changeling child—missing from the pages of the play and standing in lieu of someone or something else—does not make for a positive presence. And this lack of a positive presence resonates with two questions that Alain Badiou asks in his *Metapolitics*. First: Is it "possible to think *subjectivity without a subject*" (64)?[8] A version of this question might have been designed specifically with Shakespeare in mind, since it echoes so radically John Keats's description of Shakespeare's "negative capability"—the ability to think everything and be nothing, to be indifferent to difference. If a subject is defined tautologically as that which embodies subjectivity, then Badiou asks if the two can ever be thought separately. Is it possible to have desire without a body? By presenting us with an absent body that is very present in the desire it generates, Shakespeare's play provides the perfect setting for thinking about this conundrum: How do we feel, recognize, and identify desire without causal reference to a material body?

Badiou's second question is how "to think thought as *thought* and not as object; or again, to think that which is thought in thought, and not 'that which' (the object) thought thinks" (27). How to theatrically represent a thought—especially a thought of desire—without immediately converting it into an object? How to theatrically represent desire without immediately producing a character on stage? How to retain the drama of desire without a body?

In his introduction to the *Norton* edition of the play, Stephen Greenblatt encapsulates the commonplace understanding of desire: "No human being in the play experiences a purely abstract, objectless desire; when you desire, you desire *someone*" (810). It seems but a short step from the idea of desiring *someone* to desiring someone's *body*, even though, as the frequent conversation about "types" makes very clear—as in "who or what is your type?"—this body is never reducible to or contained by only one person. Even in our day-to-day understandings, then, desire cannot be localized in a body. Rather, we seem to desire things as small as individual attributes, traits, and features, or as large as race, gender, and class, more than a body. "The body" is both more and less than what we desire: more because we never desire it in its entirety, and less because we want it to embody all the traits that we find attractive. Either way, desire for a body is a notoriously slippery phenomenon, since it rarely translates backward or forward into desire for a person, and even less for a person who can only be identified with that body. But this slipperiness of the body compels with even more urgency the need to produce a body that can claim and *own* desire. After all, a disembodied desire is rather like a changeling child— one never knows who the rightful owner is.

Let us, for a moment, examine this question of bodily desire from the opposite end: How *does* a body help us to feel, recognize, and identify desire? Quite clearly, it permits us to make decisions based on visible markers: gender, race, ethnicity, and ability. If we identify as homosexual, then it becomes easy to recognize a member of the "same" sex in order to assess one's level of attraction, and the same goes for all other categories of visibility. Incredibly, the overwhelming majority of the world's population tends to have *homo* relationships in this etymological sense of the word— like attracting like—whether in terms of race, ethnicity, class, or sexuality. This means that for the vast majority of us, desire traces itself along trajectories of identifiable similarities.[9] What a body "does" is tell us who to choose: making a choice in the absence of a body seems like a nonsensical, even illogical, thing to do. Indeed, the absence of a body does not allow us to know who or what to desire. It takes away from us what we like to cherish as our "choice," and in the process it allows us to see that what we used to think of as choice is not choice at all, but rather a forced consensus. We "choose" based on what we perceive certain bodies to be. By converting bodies into identifiable categories, we perform the very translation that in the play turns Bottom into an ass—we translate the constraints on our choice into choice itself, and consider ourselves lucky to be able to do so. This is perhaps why even verbal markers of identity—names, indicators of religion, political opinions—are increasingly being translated into the register of the *visible*, such as skin color, head scarves, tattoos. Verbal markers exist, and provide an identity, but that identity is not satisfying enough; it is too disembodied, too abstract, and has to be converted into a picture, an image, in order to be accessible. Almost all online romance websites insist on a photograph—not only to testify to an individual's particular looks, but also to ensure that the person matches up to the verbal description of him or herself. The valorization of the visual over the verbal in the service of *verifiable* object-choice is one of the most immediate reasons that productions of *A Midsummer Night's Dream* feel compelled to produce the Indian boy on stage and screen.

But if the body constrains rather than opens up the realm of our choice in desire, then what do we gain from having it? The obvious answer, as I have already suggested, is that we do not really want choice, what we want are constraints on choice that simplify for us which bodies do and do not lie within the realm of "our" desire. This is why clinical tests of self-identified homophobic men yield such interesting results (the subjects were repeatedly aroused by gay male porn).[10] The horror—could we call it the *jouissance?*—resulting from these tests testifies to the horror of interrupting the relation between bodies and desires. If "our" desires do not match "our" bodies, then the resulting immateriality of our identities—as gay or straight or black or white or whatever—is horrifying for two reasons. First, because of how much we invest in the causal coupling of bodies and desires; and second, because of how convinced we are that our bodies are our "selves." Bodies tell us whom and what to desire, and they tell us whom and what we desire; without a body we would neither know nor be able to explain desire.

If we turn back now to the original version of the question of the relation between body and desire—not what do bodies tell us about desire, but what does the *absence* of the theatrical body tell us about desire—then we return also to the changeling Indian boy and his present-absent body in the play. The absence of the Indian boy is clear enough for us to understand—he does not appear physically in the text—but his presence is even more crucial to comprehend. He is present, not only because his name is invoked repeatedly between Oberon and Titania, but also because this invocation highlights the desire to read his role as *cause* in the play. After all, this play, like all others, draws a connection between cause and effect such that the text has a logical structure even when it is dealing with fairies rather than human beings. Such logic does not have to be mathematically precise, but it does need to tell us, for instance, why someone has been exiled if indeed she or he has been. Or why actors would abandon their co-star when they do. Or what causes lovers to run away from family and city. Or why Othello would murder Desdemona. No matter how flimsy the cause, there has to be one. And so the Indian boy is conjured up to explain the cause of the fight between Titania and Oberon, which is also the cause of many plot twists in the play.

Except that the changeling boy does not present himself as an *embodied* cause of desire.[11] Instead of underlining the importance of causality, his absence underlines the importance of divorcing desire from a body that can be named as its cause. While plot details might need to follow the logic of cause and effect, theatrical desire does not. And so even as the boy "explains" the standoff between Titania and Oberon, he cannot explain their desire for him. The boy without a body becomes present only as a missing cause. If his presence in the play is synonymous with causality of plot, then his absence insists on a lack of causality in desire. The missing body of the changeling Indian boy is paradoxically the cause of noncausal desire in the play. Or rather, the missing object of desire suggests that desire cannot be pinned down to a cause. In this play, absence itself has a causative power in relation to desire, but this "causality" gets mystified through the phantasmatic imposition in theatrical productions of a body to make the absence present.

Indeed, if absence can be ascribed causality, then it is only in a way that unsettles the very notion of cause as originary presence. Even a cursory look at the rest of the play reveals that this is a pattern: desire in *A Midsummer Night's Dream* never follows the laws of cause and effect because there is always something missing in causal explanations of desire. For instance, when Helena begs Hermia to tell the secret of her attractiveness to Demetrius, Hermia responds by saying: "I frown upon him, yet he loves me still" (1.1.194). And when Helena obsessively follows Demetrius into the woods, the man of her dreams says:

> *Demetrius:* .... do I not in plainest truth
> Tell you I do not nor I cannot love you?
> *Helena:* And even for that do I love you the more. (2.1.200–202)

These passages do not explain desire; on the contrary, they insist on its lack of identifiable causality. In *Midsummer Night's Dream*, though much is made of the physical differences between Hermia and Helena—one is short and the other tall, for instance—that difference gets far less space than the insistence on their sameness. In the lyrical description of their love—"Two lovely berries moulded on one stem" (3.2.211)—and even before, they are described as being absolutely identical: "Through Athens I am thought as fair as she" (1.1.227), notes Helena. Their bodies are not differentiable enough to provide the answer to the question of why one man might prefer one of them over the other; their bodies do not provide the much-sought-after *cause* of love.

Even more, and like Shonibare's mannequins, the physicality of appearance is repeatedly rendered suspect as a means of identification in the play. When upbraided by Oberon for having anointed the wrong man with the love juice, Puck says in his defense:

Robin: Believe me, king of shadows, I mistook.
Did not you tell me I should know the man
By the Athenian garments he had on? (3.2.348–50)

In this text, the body suggests not only a lack of differentiation—Lysander and Demetrius look startlingly alike, down to the clothes they wear—but also a lack of causality as the basis on which to understand desire. Hermia's preference for Lysander over Demetrius seems inexplicable to everyone. Demetrius's preference of Hermia over Helena seems inexplicable. Titania's "choice" of Bottom with his ass's head is absurd. And Hippolyta's "choice" of Theseus seems unmotivated. Bodies in the play do not explain or cause desire—if anything, the *absence* of bodies foments the most intense and consequential desire in *A Midsummer Night's Dream*. The absent body plots the play for us and agrees with Theseus's dismissal of the imaginary body conjured up to explain desire. This dismissal marks a break from, and interrupts, our normal association of causality among bodies, selves, and desires. For Alain Badiou, "All resistance is a rupture with what is. And every rupture begins, for those engaged in it, through a rupture with oneself" (7). *A Midsummer Night's Dream* has already provided rich material for queer theorists who have investigated the various permutations of desire—animal, lesbian, adolescent, Amazonian—presented in the play. But the text's insistence on the nonmaterial basis of desire presents us with a mode also of theorizing queer indifference.

Specters of Theater

Despite not appearing as a character in either the Folio (1623) or Quarto (1600) editions of the play, the changeling boy has been a fixture on the *Midsummer Night's Dream*'s stage from the beginning of its production history. Indeed, one might argue that his backstory is so well fleshed out in the text that it remains only to give him a local bodily habitation for him to come to life. Currently one of Shakespeare's most frequently performed plays, *A Midsummer Night's Dream* was never seen in its entirety between 1642 and 1840.[12] Instead, directors broke off chunks of the play as it pleased them—in 1716 and 1745 the play became *Pyramus and Thisbe*, in 1755 *The Fairies*, and in 1661 *The Merry Conceited Humours of Bottom the Weaver*. But the most spectacular production was that of Purcell's *The Fairy Queen*. There are no records to indicate whether or not this was the boy's first appearance, but it is the first recorded one—according to Gary

Jay Williams, "We can firmly establish the presence of the Indian boy on stage in Purcell's 1692 opera" (24)—and also the most colorful. Suggesting that their love of spectacle would not have allowed theater companies to miss out on the "opportunity to use an attractive child, at least in an early scene," Williams gives us details derived from a variant issue of the libretto: "Titania enters first, 'leading the Indian boy, fairies attending.' When a sentinel enters to warn that Oberon is coming, she commands the earth to open and receive the Indian boy. Judging from the next stage direction, 'He sinks,' it did. Oberon then enters in perplexed pursuit of the boy" (47). In 1816, Frederic Reynolds's operatic adaptation of the play elaborately staged the journey of the Indian boy from India to England, and his handover to Oberon.[13] These intricately staged renditions of the changeling boy seem eager to make physically material what the play has already given us in rich narrative detail. However, if this is indeed the case, then we are hard pressed to explain why performances that cut out the boy's narrative backstory continue to produce him as a material character on stage.

In several nineteenth-century productions, for instance, the play's account of Titania's attachment to the boy and to his mother is excised. Without these lines the centrality of the changeling boy to the play is in jeopardy, and the mystery surrounding Titania's relationship with her votaress is removed. The passage is crucial to thinking about desire in Shakespeare's text, since it gives us two absent bodies and the heated desire nonetheless generated by them. This exchange between Oberon and Titania begins with Titania's complaint that their dissension has thrown the entire world— seasons, people, everything—into turmoil. Oberon, in turn, retorts sharply:

> Do you amend it then; it lies in you:
> Why should Titania cross her Oberon?
> I do but beg a little changeling boy,
> To be my henchman. (2.1.17–20)

To which Titania responds:

> Set your heart at rest:
> The fairy land buys not the child of me.
> His mother was a votaress of my order:
> And, in the spiced Indian air, by night,

Full often hath she gossip'd by my side,
And sat with me on Neptune's yellow sands,
Marking the embarked traders on the flood,
When we have laugh'd to see the sails conceive
And grow big-bellied with the wanton wind;
Which she, with pretty and with swimming gait
Following—her womb then rich with my young squire—
Would imitate, and sail upon the land,
To fetch me trifles, and return again,
As from a voyage, rich with merchandise.
But she, being mortal, of that boy did die;
And for her sake do I rear up her boy;
And for her sake I will not part with him. (2.1.121–37)

Titania's response to Oberon gives us the entire story of the changeling boy and his mother; its excision removes the narrative details that present the boy in the play. Trevor D. Griffiths suggests that one reason for this censorship could be propriety (the votaress is pregnant out of wedlock), and another could be colonialism (productions may not have wanted to humanize Indians while busy with the national project of also subjugating them). Gary Jay Williams agrees with this latter explanation: "In nineteenth-century productions ... the presence of the Indian boy become[s] more problematic, not only because this passage is cut ... but also because of the context of the unmistakable scenic images of empire the pictorial stage will provide" (24–25).[14]

And so the votaress disappears, but the boy appears. It is crucial to note that of the cast of two absent characters in the play, one is routinely forgotten and the other is regularly made present. Even if part of the explanation for this might lie in the fact that early productions felt it violated theatrical decorum to show an unmarried pregnant woman on stage, the more important factor, I think, is that the votaress is not the subject of desire between Oberon and Titania, and therefore does not need to be made material. Titania's desire for the votaress does not translate into desire in and for the play; instead, the changeling child becomes the unseen scene of debate, the unmarked remark between Oberon and Titania. That almost no production of the play is complete without the production of the Indian boy—whether or not the lines about his lineage make it to the stage—attests to the anxiogenic nature of objectless desire. If Titania and Oberon want the boy, then we need to know what he looks like. It also suggests the lack of necessity in providing desire with a backstory: as long as desire has a visible object, it can be understood. Narrative plays a secondary role in thinking about desire, especially, it would seem, when that desire is being presented on stage.

These ideas raised by the absent body undergird the text of the play. As Barry Waller points out, "The fact of embodiment is an obvious resource to a playwright: the audience will grant at least the existence of his character before a word has been spoken" (67). But, he goes on to add, "Shakespeare nevertheless finds a range of other ways in which to express his suspicion of the corporeal—or more broadly, the visual—and the literal mindedness into which it betrays those who trust it" (69).

NONMATERIAL DESIRE

Posing insistently the question of what causes desire and how we can recognize it, *A Midsummer Night's Dream* suggests daringly that desire is indifferent to identity. Desire also does not allow objects to contain it. In making this suggestion, Shakespeare seems to anticipate in his own theatrical vocabulary Badiou's query to philosophy: "How can a philosophy be established within a theory of the *objectless* subject, while holding firmly to the demands of rationalism, i.e. of materialism"?[15] Materialization would seem to be the bottom line for any understanding of subjects and objects of desire. But in *A Midsummer Night's Dream* (and in plays like *Romeo and Juliet* with the disembodied Rosaline, and *The Two Noble Kinsmen* with the absent Flavina), it is precisely this materialization of desire that is absent. One could argue that it is only the bodily materialization that is missing. In the text, the subject is present as a name or title—the Indian boy / changeling child. But can a name confer subjectivity? Can "the (simple) name [rather be] that which 'opens up' thought, and which must be maintained throughout the investigation, without ever being 'objectified' by a definition or a referent" (*Metapolitics*, 29)? What exactly would it mean to maintain a name without defining it, to name a character without materializing it? In a very real sense, each character on stage always has two bodies: that of the actor and that of the character. The character's body remains shadowy—it cannot exist as an independent ontological entity. By not bringing the boy's body on stage, the play theorizes "character" itself as the thing that *does not ever have a body*. To understand "character" as an ontological thing is to understand it as disembodied: "character" is another word for that being whose body is always absent and for whom this absence is a condition of existence. In this sense, no "character" can ever be materialized on stage as a body. Shakespearean theatricality, then, names that condition of desire in which the body is nonmaterial. Theatrical desire neither confers subjectivity nor materializes objects.

Indeed, it also makes murky the very distinction between subjects and objects. If we are used to thinking of subjects as human beings with agency and objects as inanimate goods (or unlucky human beings) devoid of agency, then Shakespeare's use of the changeling boy calls that distinction into question. Who or what is the changeling boy? A subject with agency who causes strife in the world of fairy, or an object on which unwanted attention is concentrated? What or who are Oberon and Titania: subjects who have sway in the fairy world, or objects helplessly in the grip of desire for the Indian boy?[16] *A Midsummer Night's Dream* disturbs the distinction between subjects and objects in the realm of desire, just as it also unsettles distinctions of form (high and low) and genre (comedy and tragedy) and person (human and nonhuman). As these muddled distinctions suggest, desire in *A Midsummer Night's Dream* seems to possess the ability of converting subjects into objects and vice versa. The unseen boy has a powerful effect in the play, while Oberon and Titania seem to spin out of control. If we assume that desire confers subjectivity, then the play argues that, far from granting agency, it turns subjects into objects. The "simple name" or title does not confer subjectivity; in this play, desire implies both subjection to its whims and an absent object. Far from presenting subjects as people who desire objects, Shakespearean theatricality insists that desire can never be seen, recognized, or controlled, and that its contours can never fully be fleshed out. In the play it is this nonmaterializable desire that has the most agency of all.

Just to tantalize us even further, the play repeatedly specifies the coordinates within which the changeling boy can be found while simultaneously insisting on the boy's absence from the cast of characters. He is a "changeling" boy from "India": by providing him with a local habitation and a name, the play seems to make concrete what it nonetheless does not embody. Indeed, both these locations are notoriously unlocateable. To "be" a changeling might seem to confer a mantle of ontological legitimacy, but that ontology is presented as always already lost—a changeling, after all, is not who he is taken to be because he has been exchanged for another body. And the "India" to which the play repeatedly refers was imagined in

Shakespeare's day to be, variously, in South Asia, Indonesia, the Americas, and Ethiopia—the so-called Indian boy could be what we would understand today as Indian, Indonesian, American, or African.[17] The text gives us a changeling Indian boy who cannot be located with any precision and refuses to be embodied. To then *produce* the boy as cause, changeling, Indian, and object of desire literalizes what the play insists we read nonliterally and nonmaterially. For Shakespeare's *Midsummer Night's Dream*, desire *must* be disembodied. Only then does it qualify as desire.

Of Cause

If the body can no longer anchor desire, then we have a gaping hole where once there was a cause. If a body is withheld from the scene of desire—indeed, if desire is generated *because* of such a withholding—then we have nowhere to look in order to explain desire and how it works. It is not only the comedies, though, that present us with such a desire for the cause of desire. In Shakespeare, desire travels universally. It crosses generic, national, imaginative, conceptual, sexual, borders. Its concerns crop up at different places and times, in different texts, in connection with different pleasures, and through different genres—its milieu is migratory. If a comedy like *A Midsummer Night's Dream* insists on the nonliteralization of desire, then a tragedy like *Othello* continues to try and explain desire even after being warned off such a pursuit. This excessive desire to explain desire is what constitutes its tragedy. And such tragedy persists not only in *Othello* but also in rewritings of the play.

In Tayeb Salih's 1966 novel, *Season of Migration to the North*, Jean Morris's death revisits Desdemona's murder from *Othello* but ties its desire even more explicitly to the travails of travel. Like Shonibare, Salih too writes about the postcolonial condition in terms of the ravages of desire; like Shonibare, Salih too picks out the strands of desire woven into the fabric of travel. Mustafa Sa'eed crisscrosses lands even more than Othello does—from his village to Khartoum to Cairo to London and back to a Sudanese village. He desires even more women, and causes the deaths of at least two in addition to the one he murders. In a scene that raises to a different order of intensity the question of desire posed in *Othello*, Mustafa slowly and sensuously slides a blade in between Jean's breasts and kills her. As she gasps—for breath, with pleasure—she begs him to come with her, and he is forever filled with regret that he did not. Where Shakespeare's play dramatizes the idea that desire and death are intertwined, Salih's novel also makes explicit that it cannot adduce a reason for this mortal coil. Why does Mustafa kill Jean, and why does he kill her in bed?

This scene of murder is horrific and desirous all at once—horrific because drenched in desire—and it is the main reason why *Season of Migration to the North* is banned so widely and frequently. Indeed, its analogous scene of death in *Othello* has proved agonizing for generations of readers. H. H. Furness, for instance, admits: "I do not shrink from saying that I wish this Tragedy had never been written. The pleasure, however keen or elevated, which the inexhaustible poetry of the preceding Acts can bestow, cannot possibly to my temperament, countervail, it does but increase, the unutterable agony of th[e] closing scene."[18] The closing scene of the play—act 5, scene 2—is when Othello murders Desdemona, and where the folly of Othello's behavior unfolds after the murder has been committed. But what makes this scene "unutterabl[y]" agonizing? After all, several Shakespeare plays end with murder and bloodshed—one can think of *Macbeth* and *Hamlet*, to name only two. Why does Othello's murder of Desdemona excite more agony than, say, Laertes's murder of Hamlet?

There is one fairly obvious answer to this question: historically, patriarchal structures have allowed, indeed condoned, the killing of women by men. Sexual crimes—murders over alleged infidelity, rapes, "honor" killings—are among the most horrific of these crimes that patriarchy sanctions. There is no doubt that Othello is interpellated in just such a patriarchal structure of violence—no surprise that he finds it easy to kill his wife, no shock that such easy violence evinces agony for many of us. But surprisingly, even as the play allows us to acknowledge this historical structure of violence, it does not allow us to use it as the reason for Desdemona's murder. If anything, the play suggests that to look for a cause of Desdemona's murder (as though *any* cause could explain or condone it) is to participate in the violence unleashed by Othello against his wife. Instead, it suggests that the agony of the final scene in *Othello* derives from the fact that the play repeatedly refuses to give us a cause for it: the cause of the final scene's agony is the causelessness of the final scene. Or rather, the final scene presents a queer cause that removes causality from the realm of ontological certainty—a progenitor that explains its offspring—or logical explanation—if *x*, then *y*—and propels us instead into an absence that is foundational.

For Badiou, this absence is foundational both to the subject and the desire that marks its subjectivity; it refuses both to ground the subject and explain its particular desire: "There is no doubt that universalism, and hence the existence of any truth whatsoever, requires the destitution of established differences and the initiation of a subject divided in itself by the challenge of having nothing but *the vanished event* to face up to."[19] The subject is undone by the event because the event untethers the subject from all the markers by which it once used to be identified. Such a subject is doubly divided because the event that has undone it is not accessible as a particularity. Even as the subject might seek after the "vanished event" in order to find itself again, Badiou insists that the event is less an originary cause and more an absence that is foundational; it is lost to ontologizing quests because an event implements an *un*grounding of the self. As such, the only demand exerted by this evental universalism is that differences be disestablished, that they no longer be allowed to set up a subjective establishment. Thus, the subject that has been subjected to the de-ontologization of the event can only realize itself as an effect without a cause. The subject is divided between a memory of the difference in which it used to live and the current dispensation that dispenses with such difference as cause. Even though for Saint Paul the event is the resurrection of Christ, Badiou makes it clear that the event is not in itself a thing. Indeed, it need not be a historical occurrence at all: "Let us emphasize once more that . . . the event that [Paul] takes to identify the real *is not* real (because the Resurrection is a fable)."[20] Even more, an event is that which allows us to see effect without cause, difference without causality, division without substance. The evental subject emerges as and in the mode of desire—unmarked, restless, and finding cathexis without searching for ontology.[21] The event divides the subject from ontology by introducing it to desire; from now on, the subject is marked only fleetingly, cruising the theater of desire without settling on the ontology of causal identity.

I want to think of the event, then, less as something that can be seen and known *as* the event. Rather, the event is that—incident, moment, thought, sentence, act, history, culture, revolution—which throws into disarray our modes of knowing. The paradox of the foundational absence argues for a change that cannot be anchored; the event necessitates difference but in the mode of indifference; it universally asks questions but refuses all final solutions. In *Othello*, that evental moment comes just before Desdemona's murder, when Othello explicitly addresses the question of causality and desire. This event can neither be identified as an event except retrospectively, nor can it be witnessed. But what this evental moment does in the text is make superfluous our explanations for desire. Not only is there no explanation for desire in the play, but also there *can be none.* The event of Desdemona's murder in the last scene of the play is unutterably agonizing because it asks for a cause that we can describe as vanished, but only because it has never been there *as* cause; it is, instead, something to which we have no access but around which the play nonetheless pivots. The name for that vanished event in the play is desire—that which cannot be located but that nonetheless transforms our relation to ontology.

OFF COURSE

As we shall see, there seem to be two universal characteristics of desire in this Shakespearean tragedy: first, desire cannot provide cause; it does not have explanatory power. And second, desire itself is not caused; it does not have an origin. Desire can neither be, nor have, a cause even as it always has effects. The mistake we make is to turn back at the end of that loop and ask what causes these effects of desire. Let me be clear that not being able to pinpoint the cause of desire in no way condones the noxious effects that desire can often unleash—and does in this play. But one of the questions posed by *Othello* is whether we can move away from the expectation that desire must *have* a cause, which is an apparatus that provides an explanation. Can the subject be in the grip of a desire that insists on the "vanished event" as the ground for its being and refuses to provide a single cause for desire even as it might serve up several? Penal codes around the world lessen the punishment for "crimes of passion" because they have to do with desire. But such mitigation depends on the assumption of a lack of *intentionality*, which in turn is based on pinpointing desire as a cause that simply cannot be controlled. It is this close bond between cause and effect that *Othello* tries to disrupt. Othello's murder of Desdemona might have been a crime of passion, but its effect is agonizing and should only be treated as such. Indeed, this is what the play suggests by allowing Othello to kill himself as the horror of his deed dawns upon him. But even more crucially, the play separates cause from desire. Desire is not the explanatory cause of Desdemona's murder; rather, desire is that which does not have a cause. To seek to "explain" Desdemona's murder, then, by citing desire as its knowable cause is to ignore the powerful effects that desire has, effects made all the more powerful for not leading us back to a cause.

Indeed, this desire for causality has a history in the play itself. After Cassio has given her Desdemona's handkerchief to copy the work, Bianca exclaims: "O, Cassio, whence came this? / This is some token from a newer friend. / To the felt absence now I feel a cause" (3.4.205–7). Cassio, when he learns at the end of the play that Othello has colluded in the plan to murder him, says, "Dear General, I never gave you cause" (5.2.351). The text repeatedly tries to understand the cause of actions, the motive for passions, and the reason for disasters. And each time it comes up with nothing. Even so seemingly straightforward a plot device as the attack by the Turks early in the play is repeatedly removed from both cause and course—we are given conflicting reports about the number of their ships and the destination of their trajectory. Yet the more the Venetian senators are faced with this uncertainty, the more pompously they exclaim, "'Tis certain, then" (1.3.50). The search for a certain cause, so prevalent in the play, is again thwarted at the end when Iago refuses to explain the cause of his actions: "Demand me nothing. What you know, you know. / From this time forth I never will speak word" (5.2.355–56). *Othello* ends with a vanished event, and with questions that continue to remain unanswered: Why does Iago lie to Othello? Why does Othello believe him? Why does Desdemona allow herself to be killed? Why does Desdemona desire Othello rather than Roderigo? Why does Emilia desire to please Iago despite disliking him? Why does Iago hate Othello as much as he does?

In this play, and in each of these instances, not knowing the cause—indeed, wondering if there ever can *be* a cause—is of paramount importance. So much so that even Iago's attempts at communicating the cause of his hatred of Othello have drawn flak from his critics, prime among them Samuel Taylor Coleridge. Commenting on the unclear relationship between (Iago's) cause and action, Coleridge says that Iago is Shakespeare's only presentation of "utter monstrosity," because it "depends on the … absence of causes." But that in itself is insufficient reason to dislike Iago; rather, he is to be disliked because he performs the "motive-hunting of motiveless malignity. … In itself fiendish."[22] Instead of faulting Iago for *being* motivelessly malignant (as is commonly understood), Coleridge blames him *for* hunting after motives, for seeking causes where none might exist; in other words, for not sufficiently accepting the motivelessness of his malignity. According to Coleridge, Iago should embrace motiveless malignity, not look to cure it, because his particular brand of malignity can only *be* motiveless. In this, and without knowing it, Coleridge echoes in relation to malignity Badiou's insistence on the vanished event of desire, that which is never reducible to, or explained by, causality.

Indeed, because it cannot be identified with certainty—neither Brabantio nor Othello seems to know where Desdemona's desire lies, for instance—and because it cannot be contained within set parameters, whether of marriage or family, desire provides fertile ground for Iago's machinations in the play. Does a reading of causeless desire in *Othello* therefore automatically become an Iago-ist reading? Perhaps, though not for that reason embodied by Iago alone. Othello, for instance, enters the "unutterably agon[izing]" last scene of his play with these words: "It is the cause, it is the cause, my soul. / Let me not name it to you, you chaste stars. / It is the cause" (5.2.1–3). He has determined to kill Desdemona after believing Iago's version of her infidelity. But what *is* the cause to which he is referring here? Is it the account of Cassio's dream that Iago has fabricated? Is it an internalized racism that has convinced him he cannot hold Desdemona's desire for long? Is it Desdemona's alleged infidelity?

No matter what the cause of Othello's murderousness, it is presented in this scene as having something to do with desire. Equally, the text suggests here and elsewhere that desire *cannot* spell out its cause. This sort of paradox is not new in Shakespeare, but given its larger ramifications for how we continue to think about desire, it is interesting to parse it. Othello refuses to spell out the cause that he nonetheless invokes in triplicate. The effect of desire—if we think of Othello's crime as a crime of passion—is presented to us literally as being the consequence of a vanished event. No cause of desire, even as three causes are invoked to try and explain it. What is fascinating about this pre-murder speech is that it presents nakedly to us desire's resistance to being made the basis of epistemology, let alone ontology. Not only does this causeless desire suggest that we do not know the reason why Othello murders Desdemona, but it also argues that no matter what his reason might be, desire cannot be formulated as its basis. Othello might well have suspected Desdemona of sexual infidelity, but the event on the basis of which Othello is convinced of Desdemona's faithlessness is literally a vanished event in the play—no one sees it. Indeed, desire is never seen on stage in *Othello*—whether it be Othello's wooing of Desdemona, or Emilia's alleged affair with Othello—it is always enacted offstage. There is something ob-scene about desire in this text; it never shows its face even as the effects of desire drench the world of the play.

Even more interesting for a discussion of epistemology is that in this scene Othello seems to assume that the audience already *knows* the cause to which he refers, which is why he can depend on being understood without having to make his meaning plain.[23] The text has given us several options about the cause of desire, and we will pick one. The only option we will not pick, which is also the most agonizing one, is no cause at all.

We will always *presume* a cause that can explain desire rather than acknowl-edge a vanished event that removes the ground of desire's very being. Whether it is the patriarchal setting of the play, Iago's rhetoric, or a preva-lent belief in female infidelity, cause in *Othello* is no longer about ontology or epistemology. It cannot be conjured up in the service of knowledge because it is always the thing that exceeds the knowable. But equally, it is also what passes as knowledge in the event of desire. The audience might think it *knows* the cause—surely something that has been repeated thrice must have some foundation?—but what it knows is its desire for a cause of desire.

In its more general suspicion of causality, the play insists in particu-lar that desire can take no recourse to cause. When Othello very publicly starts acting impatiently and irrationally toward Desdemona, for instance, she simply cannot understand the reason why. Later in conversation with her mistress, Emilia broaches what seems to be increasingly obvious:

> Pray heaven it be
> State matters, as you think, and no conception
> Nor no jealous toy concerning you.
> DESDEMONA: Alas the day, I never gave him cause!
> EMILIA: But jealous souls will not be answered so.
> They are not ever jealous for the cause,
> But jealous for they're jealous. It is a monster
> Begot upon itself, born on itself. (3.4.175–83)

Emilia's conception of jealousy suggests it does not have a cause. Even though she begins her speech by looking for an *alternative* cause to the one that seems most apparent—politics rather than sexuality—Emilia ends the conversation by saying it is futile to look for a cause in matters of jealousy. For Emilia, trying to pin down jealousy's cause is an impossi-ble endeavor because jealousy is always in bed with desire. As such, one can never tell whether it has no cause or one too many: political intrigue? sexual slight? neither? both?

So what *is* the cause of which Othello boasts in the play's final scene? By way of addressing this question, let us consider briefly what Freud has to say about a neighbor who borrows a kettle and is then accused of having returned it with a hole. According to Freud, the accused neighbor comes up with three contradictory explanations: first, that he never borrowed the kettle; second, that the kettle did not have a hole in it when it was returned; and third, that the kettle already had a hole in it at the time of being borrowed. For Freud, this is a classic example of overdetermination—when no one reason will suffice to explain an occurrence and so multiple reasons are adduced for it. Overdetermination draws attention to a psychic need for causal meaning that provides too many meanings even and especially when there isn't even a single one. Each of the three explanations for the damaged kettle is plausible in itself, but the three together are mutually contradictory. The more one tries to pin down causality, the more it seems to boil away. Freud's interest in all this hot air is psychic: How does one fix identity? Every identitarian cause seems to require another one to make it more secure. Freud's point, of course, is that such security can never be achieved. This is less a moral claim and more an indicator of how the desire for a cause of desire takes us further away from, rather than closer to, causality. In Badiou's formulation, "[O]ne of the phenomena by which one recognizes an event is that the former is like a point of the real . . . *that puts language into deadlock*."[24] If the event is that which causes causality in its traditional sense to fail, then for Badiou that failure is manifested by the failure to mean. The self is no longer the self it once was; the differences by which it was once known in the world no longer compute.

Othello ratchets up the tension at which this "point of the real" is put into deadlock by adding to a verbal lie the biblical association of lying with desire. Attempting to provide Othello with proof of his wife's infidelity, Iago reports a conversation he allegedly has had with Cassio:

> OTHELLO: What hath he said?
> IAGO: (Faith,) that he did—I know not what he did.
> OTHELLO: What? What?
> IAGO: Lie–
> OTHELLO: With her?
> IAGO: With her—on her—what you will.
> OTHELLO: Lie with her? We say "lie on her" when they belie her. Lie with
> her—(Zounds,) that's fulsome! (4.1.36–45)

Led expertly by Iago, Othello makes the inevitable link here between lying as sexual act and lying as telling an untruth; to add to the epistemological deadlock, he also throws in a third intensified version of lie with "belie." The lie of language is about the act of desirous lying; the lie of language is that desire has a cause. In this play, the excess (and therefore paucity) of causes is paralleled only by the failure of the excessive "lies" that try to explain and provide cause. The play knows that the vanished event of desire cannot provide knowledge. But its protagonist in this passage is unable to understand that a superabundance of desire leads only from and to a lack of causality.

Iago generates yet another version of the Freudian kettle story when he tries to explain his animosity toward Othello ("I do hate him as I do hell (pains)" [1.1.171]). First, in conversation with Roderigo, he refers to the fact of Cassio having been promoted to the rank of lieutenant over him, then he simply repeats to Roderigo: "I have told thee often, and I retell thee again and again, I hate the Moor" (1.3.407–8). And then he lies about lying: "I hate the Moor, / And it is thought abroad that 'twixt my sheets / 'Has done my office. I know not if 't be true / But I, for mere suspicion in that kind, / Will do as if for surety" (1.3.429–33). This situation of multiple causes is at odds with the one in Shakespeare's supposed source, Cinthio's Gli Hecatommithi, in which the Iago character lusts after Desdemona and his plan to bring down both the Moor and Desdemona stems from her rejection of his advances. In Cinthio, Iago has a cause-and-effect relation to desire—Desdemona spurns his desire and therefore he desires to have her dead. In Shakespeare's play, Iago's several utterances, his multiple causes, caused Coleridge to inveigh against the villain's "motive-hunting." None of the causes adduced by Iago is the whole truth because in the play the truth of desire cannot be found. We do not even have an event from which to trace the beginning of his villainy; the event, like the cause, is always a vanished one. And though the list of his causes begins with a professional slight, it quickly devolves into sexual suspicion and then remains there. The trajectory of Iago's "cause" moves ineluctably toward the malignancy of desire, no matter how much and with what justification he tries to present it as being noble. Like the borrower of the kettle, the more Iago tries to stop up the holes in his logical apparatus, the more he betrays an excessive lack of causality in desire.

OF COURSE

Both Iago and Othello, then, share one thing in common: they both speak much too much and convey very little. This very little, though, is a reconfiguration of the standard narrative of cause-as-logical-explanation. It generates effects that can never specify their antecedents. We cannot even say that Othello's gulling by Iago such that he determines to murder Desdemona is the causal event of the play after which everything changes, because there is nothing epistemologically or experientially new about that episode. If anything, Iago is able to tap into a centuries-old patriarchal conviction about female infidelity that Brabantio too has invoked earlier in the play. Anticipating what would later become Thomas Rymer's invectives against the play, Iago's gulling of Othello only extends a suspicion that the play has had all along—that one can never tell what storms desire will unleash upon the world.[25]

From the beginning of the text, Othello and Desdemona's desire is presented as dangerous, crossing boundaries of the self as identified by race and class. But soon that danger comes to mark desire as such in the play. So it is that Othello murders Desdemona on the suspicion that she has been unfaithful to him. *And* that she might be unfaithful to other men in the future. This part of his speech—Yet I'll not shed her blood, / Nor scar that whiter skin of hers than snow, / And smooth as monumental alabaster. / Yet she must die, else she'll betray more men (5.2.1–6)—is thus both oddly personal and impersonal. My wife has betrayed me, but even more, she might betray nameless and faceless other men. The cause of Desdemona's murder is simultaneously very close and far removed, immediate and distant, personal and universal. Desdemona's desire both does and does not belong to Othello. And this is why he murders her.[26] The queer interest of this play, however, does not lie in the fact that Desdemona is murdered, but rather because both Othello's gulling and Desdemona's murder point to the indifference of desire, the remainder that resists ontological containment even after all causes have been laid bare. No matter how many reasons Othello lines up to explain Desdemona's murder, they will never be enough. And no matter how many reasons Iago gives for hating Othello, they do not add up. This is why the murder scene in the play is so unutterably agonizing—not because Desdemona is murdered, but because there is no cause that can explain her murder. Othello fears that Desdemona's desire is excessive, but then again, so is his own. Indeed, it is the ubiquitousness of excessive desire from which Othello turns away his face in this last scene.

Lest this excess be folded back into placebos about the "mysterious workings" of the heart—desire cannot be understood because it is ineffable—with which we continually bombard ourselves, let me hasten to add that, for Othello, the working of desire is less ineffable than inevitable. A causeless desire may not have an origin, but it has a destination, and it is to keep that destination at bay that we fabricate lies about love lasting forever, until death do us part. This destination is what I have been terming "indifference." The death that desire causes is the death of ontology, of a self, of two selves that can be sutured together. This is a death that is not caused at all because it asks us to move away from cause as explanation. It is also not a death in the nihilistic sense: far from saying that death is all there *is*, it heralds only the death of the fixed, explained, and ontologized self, which is to say, of the self that *never* was. If Badiou suggests that universalism disallows modes of identification—Greek, Jew—that might have operated in a different dispensation, I want to add that in an indifferent world, a subject identified by desire can no longer use desire as an identificatory cause. What *Othello* underscores about desire—causeless and unutterably agonizing—is its indifference. And it is to keep this indifference away that we reject its universal reach. Whether its senseless pulsation throbs in Desdemona's desire to have Othello, Iago's desire to be Othello, Othello's desire to save his honor, or our desire to avert the agony of the last scene, we generate as protection against the indifference of desire our desire to make sense of it. Desdemona thinks she understands Othello's appeal—"I saw Othello's visage in his mind" (1.3.251)—Iago is sure he understands his own motives, Othello is convinced he understands the extent of Desdemona's infidelity, and we assume we understand the play. To a certain extent, this is true of all desire that wants to believe that desire can be explained causally. But *Othello* turns the screws on us much more agonizingly, giving us multiple causes for desire all the while knowing that it can only end with the thrice-repeated, thrice-empty "cause." It is not Othello or Desdemona or Iago, then, who agonizingly embodies indifference in the play; it is desire itself that generates a universal agony. It is agonizing to give up an attachment to desire as cause; it is wrenching to accept the impossibility of an identity based on desire. Rather than waiting until we die, desire introduces (our) death into our lives, even and especially when it promises only good things. Desire kills, whether it is embodied by Desdemona or Othello or no one at all: that is its job. Thus it is that when Desdemona "comes back" to life after being murdered by Othello, when Emilia pleads with her to tell "O, who hath done this deed?" (5.2.132), she says, in an Odysseus-like moment, "Nobody, I myself" (5.2.133). It is this negation of the ontologizable self in response to a question of epistemology—who hath done this deed?—that marks the play's version of desire.[27]

This "nobody" that is the "I" is *Othello*'s version of indifference. Not that people do not exist and are not subject to and subjects of desire, but that this subject of desire is also a nobody; her body cannot support a (fixed) self. *Othello* explores an indifferent desire in which desire is always excessive and refers only to a vanished event that is as unknowable as it is excessive. Like Shonibare's mannequins, who do not care to divulge either their race or their sexuality even as they overwhelm us with colorful details about both, desire in this play keeps increasing, but it never adds up. *Othello* theorizes a universal queerness by declining to provide desire with a cause, and by presenting us instead with a vanished event we hope will provide the foundation for desire. Three queers instead of one cause: the play allows us to invert Othello's thrice-repeated formulation of "it is the cause" so that it suggests "the cause" is never "it." Desire in *Othello* removes itself from the social, legal, ontological, and epistemological good. The important deaths in the play are not the murders of Desdemona or Emilia or Othello, but a universal death in which desire murders causal identity. A universally causeless desire, owned by no one in particular, makes the play unutterably agonizing.[28]

3 Lesbians without Borders

The Story of Dastangoi

Theatre makes it known to you that you will not be able innocently
to remain *in your place.*

—Alain Badiou, "Rhapsody for the Theatre"

The dastan *(tale) of Chouboli is being performed by* dastangos *(tellers of tales)
in Delhi in October 2011. It is a tale of a princess who has vowed to marry
only the man who can make her speak four times in one night. Such a man does
indeed turn up, but she is a woman in disguise as a man. S/he tells the princess
four stories and gets her to speak four times. The two women get married to
each other. And then . . .*

Act I: History

Here, again, are bodies on stage. In India. Shakespearean bodies that do not
own their desires. These thoughts run through my head as I listen to a
dastangoi performance of *Chouboli* in Delhi in October 2011. The stage is a
minimalist one—a mattress covered with a white sheet, and two bolsters
on it, is at the center of the space. Flanking this mattress are two silver gob-
lets containing some liquid—water? wine?—that the *dastangos* sip during
their performance. The performance itself lasts for more than two hours,
with a short break in the middle. The language of the *dastan* is interchangeably Hindi, Urdu, and Rajasthani, with a smattering of English. Members
of the audience understand primarily one or two of the languages and frac-
tions of the others. But neither the lack of physical action on stage (a coun-
terpart to the missing physical bodies in Shakespeare), nor the lack of props,
nor the possible barrier of language, detracts from the enjoyment of the
audience, all of whom laugh appreciatively, shout out raucous comments,
and focus intently through the story of Shahzadi (Princess) Chouboli. The
dastangoi demands of its audience skills not unlike those demanded of
Shakespeare's first audiences: a tolerance for long speeches, a fascination

with philosophical conundrums, an ability to understand puns, a taste for sexual fluidity, a willingness to be diverted by stories within stories. How, in this day and age of instant gratification and elaborate cinematic and theatrical productions, is such an event even possible? What *is* this event that demands of the audience rapt attention while giving them only language in exchange?

Dastangoi is a Persian word describing the telling—*goi*—of a *dastan*, or story, with the *dastango* as the teller of the tale. It is a medieval Persian art of storytelling that made its way to India in the sixteenth century when the *dastan* of Amir Hamza, supposed to have been an uncle of the Prophet, was by far the most popular.[1] The Mughal Emperor Akbar (1542–1605) was so enamored of this *dastan* that he commissioned its conversion into manuscript form, which resulted in the twelve-hundred-folio-long *Hamzanama*. In the nineteenth century, the *dastan* of Hamza was commissioned to be written in Urdu as a compilation of all oral and written sources—a team of three scholars supervised work for twenty-five years to produce forty-six volumes of the *dastan*, each running to about a thousand pages. In Hindustan—an area roughly corresponding to what we now know as North India and Pakistan—the *Dastan-e-Amir Hamza* might have been the most popular, but it was only one of many *dastans* available for narration. Between the sixteenth and nineteenth centuries, other stories like the *Bagh-o-Bahar* joined the repertory from which *dastangos* could pick their tales.[2] At heart an oral tradition, *dastangoi* was never solely or even primarily reliant on manuscript—*dastan*, rather, was the name given to stories that shared a set of themes. These involved war, romance, trickery, and magic, to varying degrees, and a good *dastango* would throw all of them in a brew he would concoct for the telling. *Dastan* insists on verbal inventiveness, not only in the sometimes thousands of names devised for people and places, but also in the literary allusions to, and use of set pieces from, other genres and literary traditions.

Indeed, *dastangoi* flourishes on narrating stories within stories—the *Arabian Nights* would be a classic example of a *dastan* that relishes the interwoven intricacies of narrative, where one story leads not to a teleological end, but rather to another story that in turn leads to another. As the example of the *Arabian Nights* suggests, the unending narrative of a *dastan* is inevitably set in relation to a desire understood in some way as being unbounded, if only in the sense of being out of bounds. The intricate, open-ended narratives and metanarratives of *dastangoi* provide a map of desire and its fugitive movements in which the object of desire is not a thing to be obtained but rather an idea endlessly to be chased. Indeed, one of the ways in which *dastangoi* was denigrated in Hindustan was by being termed *bazaaru*—belonging too much to the marketplace, and by implication, to the lower realms of desire and longing. I will return to this aspect later. But for now, it is interesting to note that in nineteenth-century Delhi, every Thursday was the day designated for *dastangos* to gather on the steps of the famous Jama Masjid—the largest mosque in India, built by Emperor Shahjahan in 1658—and narrate their *dastans*. As an art form, *dastangoi* was never divorced from religion either in its setting or in its audience; if anything, the lines between practicing religion and enjoying desire were never drawn with finality. After all, *dastangoi* flourished alongside a Sufi literary and musical tradition in which a male poet expressed intense desire toward a male beloved.[3] The male beloved was considered synonymous with God, and in order to press the analogy home, the poet would often have to embark on a mode of itinerancy—traveling out of his gender, for instance, in order to narrate himself as the bride of God.

This itinerant mode of Sufi poetry is echoed in the *dastan* as it moves between realms, genders, and ideas. Borrowing one *sher* (couplet) from here, and one episode from there, *dastan* claims neither ancestry nor progeny: it emerges out of a mishmash of traditions, and leads to more of the same. Neither linguistically pure nor generically identifiable, *dastangoi* presents stories from everywhere and nowhere at once.[4] This tradition of storytelling, unlike the drama of the proscenium theater, does not demand that its audience be silent and invisible: since *dastans* were narrated in marketplaces and public chowks, audience members could walk away if bored, and shout suggestions if they fancied themselves as better storytellers. Nor does *dastangoi* require the verisimilitude often demanded of the theater. If anything, in insisting on magic as one of the key ingredients of a *dastan*, *dastangoi* flourishes on suspending what we understand as reality, forcing us to take seriously possibilities that we might otherwise not comprehend. Complicated tales, complex tropes, allegedly cheap desires—this is the stuff of which the itinerant *dastan* is made.

Much of this itinerancy has to do with the language of Urdu itself. Born in Delhi during the Delhi Sultanate in the thirteenth and fourteenth centuries, "the tree of Urdu grew in the soil of Sanskrit and [Braj] Bhasha, [and] flourished in the breezes of Persian."[5] No one knows quite when Urdu first "started," but the Sufi poet Amir Khusrau is most often acknowledged as being its progenitor. Except the language in which Khusrau wrote was not called Urdu—that name was an invention of the nineteenth century, when one of the outcomes of British rule was the growing divide between Hindus and Muslims. Until the end of the eighteenth century, Hindi and Urdu were both known as Hindustani, with precursor names like Hindavi, but after that date Urdu (from *Zaban-e-Urdū-ē-Muallā*, the language of the military camp, or the language of the residence of the elite; even in its etymology, Urdu traverses a wide range of possibilities) became the new language increasingly identified with Muslims, with Hindi understood as the tongue of Hindus; the former language was understood to have more Persian, the latter more Sanskrit.[6] Despite this enforced schism, Urdu continued to be the language of all of Hindustan until well into the twentieth century—the prime minister of India in 2012, for instance, still wrote his addresses to the nation in Urdu, since that was the language of instruction in which he, a non-Muslim, was raised. It is important to remember that Urdu was and continues to be a composite language. But increasingly, Urdu tends to be defined in opposition to Hindi: the latter is considered the common person's language, the language of Hindu-majority India, whereas Urdu is supposed to be the refined language of Muslim royalty. Hindi is ideologically inflected as the organic, earthy language that steers clear of Urdu's rhetorical "excesses."[7]

None of these contentions is true. As *dastangoi* makes amply clear, Urdu could not only have been the language of the court because *dastans* in Urdu were performed in bazaars and chowks across Hindustan and were immensely popular. And neither was it the language of Muslims alone, since it was the language of literacy all across northern India. But Hindi increasingly came to be seen as the language that grew from a single soil as opposed to an Urdu that drew inspiration from multiple sources and was promiscuous in its linguistic affiliations. Urdu cut across lines of community, religion, class, region, and even nation, and this caused no small degree of consternation to scholars. As Frances Pritchett describes it:

Consider, for example, the classic list of vices provided by the censorious Ram Babu Saksena in his *History of Urdu Literature* (1927). Saksena charges Urdu poetry with (among other sins) showing a "servile imitation" of Persian poetry that has led to its "debasement" and has made it, according to its own enumeration of the charges: (1) unreal; (2) rhetorical; (3) conventional;

(4) mechanical, artificial, and sensual; and (5) unnatural, for Persian poetry was often "vitiated and perverse." And unnatural things are of course doomed, if not already dying—for Nature is busy creating their fresh and natural replacements. It is actually kinder (as well as more prudent) to put them out of their misery, and to turn one's attention from morbid death to healthy rebirth." (159–60)

Pritchett's wonderful study of Urdu poetry in undivided India remains unparalleled as a document about language and its relation to politics. Examining in detail the denigration of Urdu for being "unnatural" in comparison with what the English considered "natural" poetry—their own— Pritchett asks: "But why? Only because the semantic dice have been loaded so heavily that the game is over before it starts. Because anything not 'natural' is, by definition, in one or another inherently negative state: it is affected, distorted, artificial, inauthentic, derivative, decadent, perverted, false. Anything not natural is, ultimately, 'unnatural'" (159).

Urdu poetry and, by extension, the language itself, started to become suspect in the eyes of moral purists who thought of it as being decadent— as the charge of "unnaturalness" makes clear. This was not only because of its enormous investment in the "play of words"—the puns and intricate metaphors that are integral to Urdu poetry—but also because it played with words, or so it seemed, in order to excite sexual frivolity.[8] Take, for example, a poem by Nazir Akbarabadi, who was a master of languages—he was reputed to know Arabic, Persian, Urdu, Punjabi, Brij Bhasha, Marwari, Purbi, and Hindvi. He was also a male poet who was made to dress throughout his childhood as a girl in order to ward off the evil eye. Dismissed often as a *bazaaru* poet (which is perhaps why his poetry has been included in the *dastan* of Chouboli that I listened to in Delhi), Nazir writes fairly explicitly about male-male desire. In the poem that follows, he re-creates a scenario involving a contest being held to decide who will be the best seducer. The narrator in the poem is caught unawares by the contest and appears in disheveled clothes. It turns out, however, that despite the unkempt appearance, he is carrying his trump card with him:

Listen friends, one day a whim struck a chieftain
To watch the skills of master seducers, to have some fun.
He ordered, let all the masters be brought—

Thus suddenly by his servants I was sought.
I was unprepared, but I did have my baby squirrel.
...

And when he saw my state, when he saw my lost look,
He wondered, "A boy how would he manage to hook?"
I knew what he was thinking, I did not have to be told.
Not in my pockets or in my waistband but in my turban's fold,
After much searching, I found my baby squirrel.
Sitting near and watching was his twelve-year-old boy,
Fairy-faced, a piece of the moon, a fair, plump toy—
Friends, the moment he saw my baby, on sight of it,
He was enchanted and demanded: "I want it, I want it,
Come on quick, I want it in my hands, that baby squirrel."
Anxious, desire driving him into an eager mood,
Friends, he came running, right to where I stood—
A hundred pleas, he begged: "Give it to me, give it to me!"
His father screamed: "Throw out the man immediately!"
How extraordinary the magic of this, my baby squirrel.[9]

Describing the boy as a fresh-faced piece of the moon (*chand ka tukda*) was widely accepted code for an object of adult male desire. The squirrel is sexually suggestive because of its shape and slipperiness, while the fact that it is a baby alludes more generally to the pederastic desire at play in the poem. The "fair . . . fairy" is immediately and urgently enamored of the baby squirrel and is seduced by the narrator despite the latter's disheveled look. Ironically, the poet manages to seduce the prepubescent son of the chieftain who had wanted to test the poet's skill in seducing young boys. And at the end of all this drama, the pose of the naïf is maintained: How can this little thing of mine, this smooth twitchy object, win a contest in seduction? How is it possible that boys should be so drawn to my, ahem, squirrel? The subject of the drama of seduction—the squirrel—is also the object with which the seduction is accomplished. And the means of that seduction is the language of the poem that invites and challenges us to read Urdu in all its multiplicities.

It is this ability to speak in a forked tongue, in a language at once sexual and ordinary, seductive and prosaic, Persian and Brij Bhasha, that is the hallmark of popular Urdu poetry. This ability indicates also an inability to pin down the language of Urdu and its politics. And once this instability was transmuted into "unnaturalness" and made applicable to Urdu culture in general, the suppression by the moral police was severe. Importantly, this condemnation of the unnaturalness of Urdu coincided with the increasingly heavy hand with which the British established its political and military hold over India. The downfall and ghettoization of Urdu started after the Mutiny of 1857, when terrible British reprisals were visited upon Delhi and its cultured Muslim elite who were thought to be in cahoots with the rebellious Mughal court. As with all acts of political violence, it was not by mass murder alone that the day was won. What happened after 1857 was a large-scale downgrading of all things "native"—especially Urdu, whose biggest achievement as a language had hitherto been to defy the dichotomy of native and foreign.

Urdu became the linguistic site of an imperial battle. Once India lost, it was introduced to notions of linguistic sparseness and morality. Independence from the British in 1947 did little to change this new Victorian mind-set that Hindustan and its Urdu culture had inherited in the middle of the nineteenth century when language was valued for its instrumentality rather than its rhetoric. As Pritchett points out, the high point of Matthew Arnold's praise of William Wordsworth's poetry was that it had "no style,"[10] and this lack was precisely what the British colonials used to elevate themselves and downgrade Urdu. Indeed, as she goes on to note:

> If [after 1857] Wordsworthian poetry was the touchstone of naturalness, [then] the whole Indo-Muslim poetic tradition was bound to appear "unnatural" in comparison—not just literarily decadent, artificial, and false, but morally suspect as well. And if, as many English writers argued, poetry was inevitably a mirror of society, then the cultural rot must go much deeper. The result was a sweeping, internally generated indictment with which Urdu speakers have been struggling ever since. (xvi)

Urdu suddenly became "unnatural," and Muslim rulers both wordy and sexually decadent: a colonial mission became fused with both a sexual and a literary one. The kingdom of Avadh, for instance, was simultaneously the last holdout against the British, and the one that the British narrated as being the most sexually deviant. Its Nawab, Nasiruddin Haider, would on "the birth date of each Imam . . . pretend to be a woman in childbirth. Other men imitated him, dressing and behaving like women during that period. British Victorian men viewed this kind of transgendered masculinity as unmanly decadence."[11] Several poets are described as having dressed as women at nineteenth-century *mushairas* in Delhi,[12] and the "play of words" that marked Urdu poetry reached a zenith with the homoerotic double entendres of its verses.[13]

If post-1857 British rule in India saw the deployment of an unprecedented degree of force in arms, then it also witnessed an implacable censoring of Urdu literature. Having internalized this censorship, Muhammad Sadiq is able to write of the *ghazal* form (composed of rhyming couplets and a refrain, not unlike that of a sonnet) in 1964 that it "envisions love as 'a torture, a disease,' a 'morbid and perverse passion'—a view that is 'a legacy from Persia' and is 'ultimately traceable to homosexual love' which had taken deep root among the Persians and Persianized Arabs.'"[14] It is striking how similar this denigration of love in the *ghazal* is to that of love in Shakespeare's sonnets. For instance, in 1793, George Steevens refused to include the sonnets in his *Complete Works of Shakespeare*: he thought them unworthy of an exalted place as a collection of literature. His disgust at sonnet 20 (in which Shakespeare addresses "the master-mistress of my passion") is quite startlingly like that of Sadiq: "It is impossible to read [sonnet 20] without an equal mixture of disgust and indignation," he states.[15] This disgust, apparently caused by the remapping of gender and desire, seems to cause great pain to these critics and so they take great pains to disavow what their poets have written: "great" poetry cannot be about "that" because "that" by definition belongs elsewhere. These nineteenth century denigrations of the "unnatural" mapped poetry onto desire and denounced both as being decadent, fanciful, and immoral. As Sadiq goes on to add: "Over time the ghazal has gone from bad to worse. It has developed 'wholly in the direction of fantasy and unreality': 'facts give way to fancies,' and the imagination explores 'curious byways' as the ghazal evolves 'in its downward career.'"

Little wonder, then, that *dastangoi* started to crumble along with the rest of the Urdu edifice. Openly disseminating wondrous tales, *dastans* were not contained either literally within a written text or physically within an acting space or metaphysically within one worldview or socially within one milieu or linguistically within one language or sexually within conventional bounds. While this very lack of codification allowed *dastangoi* to get off relatively easily in the pecking order of denigration, it nonetheless died out in the twentieth century. As Mahmood Farooqui, the leading revivalist of *dastangoi* in twenty-first-century India, argues:

Seeking to yoke literature to social reform and emphasizing purity of thought and simplicity of style, Urdu's leading critics privileged truthful experience rather than exaggerated inventions. Desirous of mirroring western, more particularly Victorian, literary values they praised moralistic and realistic fiction and long narrative poems. *Dastans*, by then, were already an object of religious censure, women particularly were advised against reading them because it would corrupt them. At the same time colonial officers found *Dastans* to be immoral and obscene. Added to this was the growing contempt of Urdu's own critics who found *Dastans* to be childish, inconsistent, implausible, and too repetitive. The only permissible fictional form for the reformers was the novel and the *Dastan* was a veritable anti-novel, not a precursor to it but quite a different form.[16]

The *dastan* offended in terms of content, and it was also literally in bad form. Neither the ancestor of the novel nor the descendant of the narrative poem, the *dastan* did not fit any formal device that could be conjured up for it. It had no fixed shape, which is perhaps why, as Farooqui goes on to argue, it merged seamlessly into the film industry that to this day remains such a craze in India and Pakistan. Incorporating Hindi, Urdu, regional and international languages, marked by fertile tropes and poetic language, using set-pieces, time-tested plot devices of intergenerational conflict, male-female relations, song and dance, and desires that do not conform to gender types, *dastangoi* is both the descendant of Shakespearean drama and the precursor of Bollywood film.

ACT II: THEATER

In suggesting that the *dastan* is "a veritable anti-novel," Farooqui uncannily echoes Alain Badiou, who makes the same claim for the theater in his essay "Rhapsody for the Theatre":

> Grappling with incompleteness, martyred by the not-all, jealous of the novel, the theatre author often wants to complete things. Anxious of being suspended from the aleatory character of an event, he jumps ahead of the game in despair. Whence the stage directions, which became almost endless in the nineteenth century, claiming to define the decor, the costumes, the gestures, the figures. . . . In actual fact, this meant an invasion of theatre by the novel, under the law of an author who would much rather make a whole out of his theatrical proposition.

The theatrical real does away with all that, it expels the novel, and it chastises the stage directions. In this sense, it comes back to the text, by freeing itself from the harmful book to which the stage directions had pinned it. (213)[17]

Badiou opposes the theater to the novel in much the same way as Mikhail Bakhtin opposed the novel to the epic. The claim in both cases is for more malleability—Bakhtin famously compared the novel to clay and the epic to marble.[18] But for Badiou, theater also names what is dangerously unending about literature, what cannot be contained within the covers of a book or the puncta of a sentence or the psychology of a character. Stage directions intervene to try and control the necessarily unfinished and unfinishable structure of theater; this intervention performs also a transformation as the theater mutates into the novel, luxuriating in all the psychological depth and narrative coherence for which the novel is famous. But literary "open-endedness" is not enough—what the anti-novel of the theater does is perform a problematic of ontology by tying itself to the specter of failure. Stage directions try and make a "whole" out of a "theatrical proposition" that fails to deliver a self-identical with its identity. The "theatrical real"—Badiou's version of the Lacanian Real that shapes the Symbolic but can never be apprehended from within it—is the point at which theater can no longer evade its failure. Far from being the real of what we think of as everyday reality, the Lacanian/Badiousian real is the point at which our fantasies of coherence fail. Theater performs this failure because it disallows the ontology of characters-as-human-beings with desires they can own and control. Indeed, Badiou suggests banning the convention of actors coming out on stage "as themselves" at the end of a play to receive audience applause because the theater can never generate either reality or teleology. "Anxious of being suspended from the aleatory character of an event," the playwright rushes to fill in all these gaps performed by and in the play. But this anxiety, as the indeterminate syntax of Badiou's sentence itself suggests, is caused not just by the open-endedness of plot and language, but also and primarily by the aleatory character of *the event*, the chance encounter that can change our ontological protocols forever.

Because it *performs* its inability to settle down, because it has to stage the gap between utterances, because being is articulated as greater and lesser degrees of fantastic performance, theater allows us to rethink the ground on which the self stands. This rethinking is the result not of an existential dilemma so much as an evental one—the question is less about the value of our existence and more about the particularity from which we speak, the attributes we give to ourselves, our identity. Can we ignore theater's assault on ontology and continue to live our lives as before, or is theater allowed to create in us an evental change that takes us out of ourselves?

In his essay, Badiou's term for and about the theater is "rhapsody," a word that has important consequences for how we think of desire. Deriving as it does from the ancient Greek *rhapsoidos*—to stitch together—a rhapsody is a "literary work consisting of miscellaneous or disconnected pieces; a written composition having no fixed form or plan" that is "exaggeratedly enthusiastic or [has an] ecstatic expression of feeling."[19] Like *dastangos*, rhapsodes were itinerant poets, often depicted with their traveling cloak and staff. They patched together narratives in the same way that Shonibare stitches his mannequin's clothes. Even while forming a whole continuous poem, these stitched-together threads also refused to cohere into one; depending on the audience, different passages would be brought to the fore and other ones deleted altogether. This rearrangement of themes and tropes ensures an unviable ontology—there is no self fixed to, or to be gained from and in, the rhapsody. The narrative form of the rhapsody and its "excessive" emotion echo the endless tales the *dastan* weaves together to produce its theater. The lack of an overarching truth combined with constant movement allows us to theorize, however unwittingly, a queer desire that insists on movement away from an ontological stability to an ecstasy, an *ex-stasis*, that cannot sit still. This ecstasy is a staple of Sufi music in which the avowed goal is to move out of one's self in order to merge with God. Even if we remove from such ecstatic poetry the religious sensibility that suffuses it, there still remains a very strong sense that we do not occupy fixed positions from which to speak. This is why Sufi poets often speak in other voices—men speak as women, the beloved teases both sexually and spiritually, the context shifts among gardens, beds, heavens. Such continual movement shatters any configuration of the self that is tempted to narrate itself as rooted. Being open to the rhapsody of the theater means never being able to speak "as a."[20] In terms of literature, this produces texts and modes that are impossible to classify generically and erotically, resistant to being fixed in place.

Take, for example, Khusrau's early Hindavi poem that continues to be one of the most popular *qawaalis* (Sufi devotional songs) in India and Pakistan today:

Chhāp tilak sab chīnnī re mose nainā milāike
Bāt agam keh dīnī re mose nainā milāike
Prem bhaṭī kā madvā pilāike
Matvālī kar līnhī re mose nainā milāike
Gorī gorī baīyān, harī harī chuṛiyān
baīyān pakaṛ har līnhī re mose nainā milāike
. . . Khusro Nijām ke bal bal jaiye
Mohe suhāgan kīnhī re mose nainā milāike.

You met my eye and snatched away my being
You made me drink wine from the distillery of love
And intoxicated me with just one look;
My fair wrists adorned with green bangles
Have been held hostage by the embrace of your look.
. . . Khusrau gives his entire being to you, O Nizamuddin,
You have made me your bride with just one look.[21]

Its obvious homoeroticism aside—Khusrau as the Sufi saint Nizamuddin's
bride wearing the green bangles of a new wife—this poem gives us a sense
of the typical Sufi desire to be anti-Statist. Not just the State as defined
by politics, but also the state of being that one might inhabit more particularly. In the drama of Khusrau's poem, men are attracted to men, man
becomes god and vice versa, a glance destroys the resistance that is the self.
Nothing remains in its place, and there are no stage directions to indicate
where that place might have been in the first place. An itinerant identity
marks both the Sufi *qawaali* and the *dastan*, and in both genres, the itinerancy is sparked by the mobility of desire. Like the *qawaali*, *Dastangoi* too
has no stage directions even when it has a manuscript; instead, it formally
opens itself up for scrutiny, and perhaps more uncomfortably, leaves us
open to be unraveled. What interests me about the *Chouboli dastan* in particular is its ability to be opposed to the S/state, all the while providing
raucous entertainment of a kind not usually associated with rocking the
status quo.

Badiou spells out the difference between what he terms good Theater—
spelled with a capital T—and theater that does not move us out of ourselves. The former is an event with consequences for being, while the
entertainment provided by the latter does not induce any change in our
ontological pattern:

The hatred of Theatre, expressed in the love of "theatre," is ultimately a form of self-hatred. We are that person who arrived for the sake of the ritual insipidness of a celebration of self, some laughs, culture, recognizable figures, feeling always one foot ahead, answers that "hit the nail on the head," sublime decors, communion during intermission. All of a sudden, sticking closely to the event's unfolding and following a set of trajectories subtracted from all calculation, we must pass through the twists and turns of desire, see the object eclipse itself before our eyes and, in the impasse of form, hit upon some incongruous point of the real. In order not to endure all this in a disagreeable commotion, and so as not to avoid it through the facile solution of boredom, there is no resource other than a willful attention and a sustained, though latent, exercise of thinking. (199)

If one usually goes to the theater to indulge in "the ritual insipidness of a celebration of self," then Theater is that which refuses to reinforce the self with which we entered the theatrical space. Theater is the mode by which the Self is forced to abandon itself. "[F]ollowing a set of trajectories subtracted from all calculation," the Theatrical self is no longer marked by the positive attributes it might once have fancied itself as possessing.[22] Instead, seared by the event of the Theater, the self becomes subtractive: it dismantles its core, shedding rather than taking on attributes.

Such a subtraction becomes Theater. If theater is to be not just entertainment, but also pose for our consideration an event that challenges our sense of ontology, then "we must pass through the twists and turns of desire, see the object eclipse itself before our eyes and, in the impasse of form, hit upon some incongruous point of the real." The incompleteness of the theatrical form must allow us to acknowledge the incompleteness of our own forms, our selves. This simultaneous incompletion and superabundance of the self, the sense that it cannot conform generically, is generated by desire: it is what allows us to lose our identity in the way Khusrau loses his to a glance from Nizamuddin Auliya. In the *qawaali*, as in the *dastan* of Chouboli, it is desire that has the ability to take us away from ourselves without depositing us anywhere in particular. Equally, the object of our desire—even and especially if that is our self—has to vanish from view so we can take seriously that vanishing point as the theatrical real, in the Lacanian sense, where desire abounds and identities fade. The theatrical self crosses chasms of desire and is pummeled by the vagaries of the crossing. There is, however, no fixed destination toward which it reaches, nor is it in pursuit of anything or anyone in *particular*. This movement without object or arrival is the very substance of theatrical insubstantiality.

ACT III: STORY

But we need a more expansive understanding of what Badiou calls the theater. *Dastangoi* does not, strictly speaking, fit the seven parameters of what counts as theater in "Rhapsody for the Theatre": "Place, text or its placeholder, stage director, actors, decors, costumes, and public are the seven required elements of theatre" (191). In its original version, *dastangoi* never had a set place of performance—it would wander about towns and markets at will. Nor did it have a stage director, because there used to be no stage as such; decor is out since the *dastango* was meant to perform the setting through his voice and intonation. Badiou provides a slightly more relaxed definition of the theater a page before the one quoted above: "Let's posit that there is theatre as soon as we can enumerate: first, a public gathered with the intent of a spectacle; second, actors who are physically present, with their voices and bodies, in a space reserved for them with the express purpose of the gathered public's consideration; and, third, a referent, textual or traditional, of which the spectacle can be said to be the representation" (190). This earlier definition does away with director and decor and allows for the possibility that the referent of the play can be tradition instead of written text—*dastangoi* would certainly fit within these parameters of theatricality. But I must add that the subject of this chapter—the *dastan* of Shahzadi Chouboli—has been written and performed in the late twentieth and twenty-first centuries, respectively, which means it operates in different conditions from those in which the *dastan* was performed in Hindustan until early into the twentieth century. In the current revival of *dastangoi*, a performance is held in an auditorium or amphitheater, bringing it closer to Badiou's stricter definition of theater. What we have today, then, are dramatic presentations of *dastangoi* rather than *dastangoi* itself. Despite narrating the same or similar stories, simulating the mode of storytelling, and having no props on stage, today's *dastangoi* is more structured in its conditions of performance than it would have been in its heyday. However, it continues to insist on narration alone: the voice and body of the actor have to command the stage or else lose the theatrical battle forever. There are no props to hand, no other characters who enter into dialogue with the narrators on stage (other than the audience, a fact to which I will turn later); everything depends on the story, its language, and its narration. *Dastangoi* insists on the basics of theater.

"Shahzadi Chouboli Boli" is the title of the *dastan* performed by Mahmood Farooqui and Danish Husain, mostly in Delhi, but also sometimes in other metropolitan cities; it has yet to embark on an itinerant tour through rural northern India, which would have been its automatic stomping grounds in an earlier age. The *dastan* announces its verbal inventiveness in the title itself with the pun on "boli"—she spoke—encoded also in the name of the protagonist, Chouboli. This titular name is performative as well—Chou boli, four speeches, is the name of the person who speaks four times; this quartet of speeches is the very condition on which the story rests. Farooqui's working script is a translation into Hindi and Urdu of Christi Merrill's English translation of noted Rajasthani author and literary activist Vijaydan Detha's quotidian Rajasthani with the help of a Rajasthani-inflected Hindi translation by Kailash Kabir.[23] As this brief itinerary suggests, the *dastan* of *Chouboli* is living up to the itinerant history that is an integral part of *dastangoi*. Not only does *dastan* travel between nations and regions, but it also and especially travels between languages—the diverse composition of Urdu is a fit enough vehicle for such a restless literary form, and with his translation of *Chouboli*, Farooqui keeps alive the patchwork of languages that marks the *dastan* as at once inventive and unidentifiable.

True to the antiteleological thrust of *dastangoi*, we never actually reach the end point of a story without simultaneously beginning a new tale—in the story of *Chouboli*, this happens four times, and even the end of the *dastan* does not seem final. Such a lack of finality echoes the mode by which *Chouboli* was written down in the first (or second, third, fourth?) place—Vijaydan Detha has written all his folk tales after listening to oral versions of the same tales, and he has no idea from where *those* have derived. According to Merrill, "He deftly combines modern literary technique with traditional storytelling convention to create written versions of stories he has heard from friends, family and neighbours" (6); indeed, he seems to insist on this unceasing movement:

> By the time I [Merrill] began working with him more closely, his concern was that we each craft the stories to make them vivid and relevant for the intended audience, so that someone else would want to pass them on. He

seemed a little irked by the metropolitan emphasis on copyright and attri-
bution to a single author. Detha told me he had heard these stories from
aunts and neighbouring potters and peasants and courtly servants, visiting
holy men and thieves. These were their stories when they told them, and
now his stories as he wrote them. How could anyone claim sole ownership?
He said that a well-narrated story could move from oral to written, back to
oral and then to written again. It could take on countless forms. (16)[24]

Rejecting the straitjacket of ownership, Detha understands that story
travels—one can even say that is its most distinctive feature. For him, only
when it travels does a story withstand the test of time and quality: *dastangoi* capitalizes on this feature and travels with its stories of travel. In
Chouboli, however, as we will see, despite the travel involved in the tale, the
movement is more notably among different ontological assumptions we
make about desire and language. Because ideas such as these can change
our relation to our self and to the world, they also attract a high degree of
hostility. Indeed, the threat of an ontological rupture is one of the primary
reasons for people's aggression toward the theater: "But Theatre demands
that its spectator, who as a result will feel the hardness of his seat, attach
the development of meaning to the lacunae of the play, and that he become
in turn the interpreter of the interpretation. Who would not detest the
fact of having paid for pleasure and being forced to perform a kind of
work? Or rather, who would not hate that this pleasure, which one would
desire to be immediate, is the doubtful product of the mind's concentrated
effort?" (199). The danger of analysis of course is that it insists on thought;
even more, it flirts dangerously with ruptures (what Badiou calls "lacunae")
that threaten to dismantle our formal identities. What is worse is that the
theater does not deliver immediate relief for the problems it raises. Instead,
it makes us sweat only to reward us at the end with a lack of ontological
grounding. For Badiou, Theater stages the event of dismantling the self.
Any moment of rest is only a pause on the road to further dissolution. This
event can occur anywhere and at any time: its only condition is that it has
the ability to change the conditions within which we live and consider our
lives; it marks a break with our present being such that we can no longer
occupy a single ontological frame. The singularity of the event does not
provide the kind of pleasure for which we believe we have paid. Indeed,
such an ontological rupture postpones pleasure because it takes the form
of desire—forever in pursuit yet never arriving.

Chouboli enacts this rupture both literally and figuratively. Existing as it does in many tongues—Rajasthani, Rajasthani/Hindi, English, Urdu/Hindi/Rajasthani—the *dastan* of *Chouboli* forces the auditor to interrupt her understanding by providing several moments of linguistic incomprehension when the language changes with lightning speed. Unlike the cinema, there are no subtitles here to help with translation, so the break performed by *Chouboli* is a very literal one. Nor can one always tell *when* the break is happening since the "different" languages are also very similar to one another. The audiences on the two occasions I saw *Chouboli* maintained both a fascinated stillness, because they were intent on the narrative, and a voluptuous rustle as each asked her neighbor the meaning of words/sentences/poems to which there was often no reply. *Chouboli* bombards us with so many languages in one story that we lose our ability to understand or delineate any one language completely—we certainly are not allowed to indulge in "the ritual insipidness of a celebration of self." Even the *recognition* of different languages does not allow us to feel in control because we are not prepared for the rapidity of the shift from one linguistic register to another. Darting also between different forms—poetry, prose, couplets, fairy tales, folklore, universal tropes of adventure and magic, popular phrases from Hindi movies—*Chouboli* refuses to give us a single genre or version in which to call ourselves our own. Its formal multiplicity insists on the impossibility of ontological finality, and its linguistic variation only extends that challenge. The multiple formal and linguistic status of *Chouboli* refuses to guarantee its own identity, let alone ours. It leaves us suspended.

Chouboli further emphasizes this quality of suspense in both its written and performed versions. Since the written version has at one point already been performed—it has been an oral narrative and a well-known folktale—and will at another point be performed again, either orally by being translated into Urdu and Hindi, or literarily by being translated into and then out of and then into English again, it both does and does not exist as theater at all points in time. If anything, this exacerbates the suspension enacted by the text as it refuses to settle into either pure play-text or enacted theater. Suspense can of course be teleological—we await a conclusion that will make sense of everything prior to it. But *Chouboli* speaks of the pleasures of suspense without a conclusion. Almost as if, developing Lacan's distinction between the goal and aim of desire, the *dastan* insists that even as the goal might be the end point, the aim or trajectory of desire does not have a necessary *telos*.[25] And true enough, despite the length and convolutions of the *dastan*, we are left uncertain about the identities of desire with which this tale ends.

Even before the end, however, *Chouboli* does not clearly demarcate the narrative engine that drives the story. We might imagine that the narrators have the reins of the story firmly in hand, but the narrators themselves insist it is the *hunkara* given by the audience that welds the story together. Described by Merrill as "the back and forth call and response" by the audience, the *hunkara* is invoked at several points in *Chouboli* to beseech the audience to allow the story to move forward: as the joint protagonist of the tale says on more than one occasion: "hunkara bin kahaani jaise namak bin khana" [a story without a *hunkara* is like food without salt] (19).[26] Later, this plea becomes increasingly elaborate:

> Jaise kajal bin aankhen, jaise sindoor bina maang, jaise preet bina preetam, jaise bindiya bin peshani, waise hunkara bin kahani. Jaise raat bin din nahin, jaise badal bin suraj nahin, waise hunkara bin kahani nahin. (39–40)
>
> Like eyes without kohl, like a woman's hair parting without vermilion, like love without a lover, like a forehead without a bindi, so too a *dastan* without a *hunkara*. Just as there can be no day without night, no sun without clouds, so too can there be no story without a *hunkara*.

The similes in this invocation are astonishing since they also double as a blazon of Chouboli: the description of her eyes, her hair, her clothes, are all yoked in the service of getting her to speak. This part of the *dastan* is a story about the telling of a story: without the *boli* of Chouboli, it will fail to materialize as a narrative. Indeed, the *dastan* is written on and as the body of Chouboli: if there is no speech, both the *dastan* and Chouboli will disappear. The sexualized body of the woman *is* the desiring voice of the *dastango*. Without a body there can be no voice. But equally, it is not the body of Chouboli that needs to speak in order for *Chouboli* to flourish. The *hunkaras* are never given by her—it is as though her identity is dispersed through her setting: whoever speaks, speaks Chouboli. In this instance, the speaker implores, but is met with a stony silence—the clouds eclipse the sun despite the plea for their necessary coexistence, and the story cannot move until a respondent comes forward.

No *dastan*, then, without a *hunkara*. We can hear this plea as mere formal condescension—something that is routinely written into the oral narrative of the *dastan*. That may well be the case, but in *Chouboli* it is also much more than the routine invocation of a well-loved folk tradition; as Dev Pathak notes:

> [Vijaydan Detha's] stories unfold in a framework with apt devices that fuse tellers and listeners, as well as readers of the book, into one entity embedded in the stories. By starting stories with nonsense rhymes or convincing readers of the significance of *hunkara* (the nods of listeners to ensure the bilateral transaction of stories), each story merges the subjectivities of listeners with those of characters in the tales. In this way, ideas of the living and dead, natural and supernatural, flora and fauna, historical and mythological, social-mundane and divine-excellence, join in a conversation that leads the tales to myriad inconclusive conclusions. Thus, at the end of each story there is an instant need to go back to the beginning for another reading and for another way of comprehending.[27]

The *hunkara* completes the *dastangoi* by keeping the *dastan* incomplete; the assumption is that as long as there is a *hunkara*, there will be another story to come after the present one. Indeed *Chouboli*'s commitment to allowing the visibility of incompletion is narrated in some of the most beautiful lines in the *dastan*. Going through her repertory of tales to try and get Chouboli to speak, the narrator arrives at the start of her fourth story within a story, and asks for a *hunkara*. The pilajota lamp offers to do the honors, but when Chouboli makes her anger evident—she turns her face away from the lamp—another voice emerges:

> Roshni ke peechhe chhupa hua andhera ab khamosh na reh saka aur bola main andhakar hun aur yahi chhipa hua hoon, roshni ke peechhe, par roshni ki wajah se tum mujhe dekh nahin pa rahe ho. Par aise adbhut aur shandar kissago ko hunkara na mile yeh to bade sharm ki baat hogi—main doonga hunkara. (60–61)
>
> The darkness hidden behind the light could keep silent no longer and said I am darkness and I am hidden in plain sight behind the light; the dazzle of the lamp prevents you from seeing me. It would be a great shame for such a marvelous and magnificent storyteller not to get a *hunkara* for his *dastan*—I will give the *hunkara* to your story.

The story then carries on, driven by the *hunkara* provided by the darkness. These interruptions to the story are part of the story, even as they are presented extradiegetically, and the irruption of the *hunkara* marks the moment at which the boundary around the story is shown up, brilliantly, for and in all its artifice. The darkness lights up the narrative, which in turn hurtles toward its unreachable destination. It is useful to note that these pleas for and responses to the *hunkara* do not involve breaking the frame of endless storytelling. Unlike "the prurient appeal to applause" (222) that Badiou condemns at the end of a stage-play, the appeal for the *hunkara* insists only on the interimbrication of narrator and audience such that neither identity gets set in cement: actors become eager audience members, while the audience takes on narrative control. *Dastangoi* cannot exist within boundaries that it does not simultaneously also obliterate.

The opening lines of the performed version of the tale begin with an invocation in Urdu from the poetry of Intezar Husain, after which the story proper starts:

> Bhagwan Ram ki kripa bani rahe taaki Chouboli ki yeh kahani bar-bar sunayi jaati rahe aur har yug aur har daur aur har mulk aur har khitte aur har quam mein iss kahani ko sunane wale aur isse sunne wale paida hote rahein. (1)
>
> May Lord Ram continue to bless us so that Chouboli's story may be narrated over and over again in every generation in every age in every realm in every region in every nation. May there always be born people to tell this tale and people to listen to it.

A brief glance at the opening sentence presents a flavor of the riches to come. The line invokes sacred figures from Hindu mythology, yet uses more Urdu words than Hindi. The endlessness of the tale, its cyclical return, and the necessity of the audience are all emphasized at the very beginning as the stage is set for the start of the tale. And thus it begins: a landlord *(thakur)* with impressive landholdings and wide sway over his lands has one very bad habit. Every morning he likes to shoot one hundred and eight arrows though his wife's nose-ring. For this purpose he has had marked two spots on the terrace of his house, one on which his wife stands, and another, a hundred and eight paces away, on which he stands in order to accomplish his feat in archery. His wife wilts in fear at her daily ordeal, and complains to the niece of the estate manager, who exclaims in shock that if *her* husband were ever to use her as target practice, she would show him what's what. The wife, unfortunately, does not dare to say this to her husband in her own behalf, and instead narrates what the manager's niece has said. The *thakur*, incensed at this challenge to his authority, and that too from a woman, demands the niece's hand in marriage so he can make her a part of his archery routine and thus teach her a lesson. The manager's niece, astonishingly, agrees to the marriage. On the first morning after the wedding, the *thakur* prepares to shoot one hundred and eight arrows through his new wife's nose ring. The newlywed wife begins to taunt her husband about his masculinity by observing that shooting arrows through a nose-ring is no big deal; indeed it is a feat she too can achieve with ease: "Yeh [Rajkumari Chouboli ka haath jeet] kar ke dikhao to main tumhari bahaduri ko manoon" [If you're able to win the hand of Princess Chouboli, then I will acknowledge your mastery] (10). It turns out that Shahzadi Chouboli has refused to marry any man except the one who can make her speak four times during the course of one night. Hundreds of princes have tried their hand at achieving this feat, but have failed to make Chouboli's tongue move. As punishment for their failure, they have been imprisoned in a dungeon and made to grind fodder for horses.

Shocked by Chouboli's taunt, the *thakur* sets off to achieve this difficult task. But like all the men before him, he fails and is imprisoned in the dungeon. Then the manager's niece goes out in male disguise to see if she can win the hand of Shahzadi Chouboli. She succeeds, of course, by narrating four gripping tales to each of which the princess feels compelled to respond, thus fulfilling the condition of speaking four times in one night. True to the terms of the agreement, Chouboli and the manager's niece get married and head back to the *thakur*'s village, with the unsuspecting *thakur* in their entourage as a servant. Taking pity on him, the manager's niece decides to set him free and allow him to take possession once again of his lands, and of his newest wife, but only after she puts him through some humiliations, and then makes clear that she and Chouboli will be the ones living together—the *thakur* is to be kept on only as their "scarecrow."

Even at first glance, it is easy—perhaps astonishing—to see how much *Chouboli* shares in common with myths and literatures from other parts of the world. The princess who sets a seemingly impossible task for her suitors only to eventually succumb to love (Atalanta), the woman dressed as a man who succeeds where no man has done before (Portia in the courtroom scene of *The Merchant of Venice*), the continual storytelling of fantastic tales meant to stave off doom (Scheherazade)—all these threads are spun into the fabric that is *Chouboli*. Added to these multinational strains are the multiple forms and languages in *Chouboli* itself, so what the audience hears and sees during the performance is a mode of narrative that not only redraws boundaries but also allows us to ask what goes into the making of a boundary in the first place. What is the difference between Greek myth and Indian folktale, between Urdu and Hindi, between women and men? Can a popular folktale end with two married women living together happily ever after? Are cross-dressing women lesbians? Is there an identity to hold on to in the swirls of all these ruptures?

Whether or not they can be identified with certainty as lesbians, Chouboli and the manager's niece are intensely attracted to each other: "Thakurayin . . . usko dekhte hee uspe fida ho gayi" [The *thakur*'s wife was smitten as soon as she looked at Chouboli] (19). After Chouboli has spoken for the second time in the story, and is thus halfway toward losing her cause, the manager's niece once again asks for the *hunkara* to be given, and Chouboli's necklace volunteers to do so. Chouboli fixes her necklace with a fierce look of disapproval, which prompts the *kissago* (teller of tales) to chide her:

> Tum se chup na raha gaya to ilzam doosron ko kyun deti ho. Kya patta mera sundar roop dekh kar tum mujh par mar mitti ho aur man hee man apni pratigya todni chahti ho. // Chouboli ne baat ka jawab na diya aur sar jhuka kar baith gayi. (51)
>
>> If you were unable to keep silent, then why blame others? Who knows, but perhaps you are so enthralled by my beautiful frame that you are secretly trying to break your vow. // Chouboli refused to answer and sat with bowed head.

There is something about Chouboli's anger that the manager's niece aka *kissago* aka *thakurayin* aka Chouboli's lascivious suitor finds irresistible:

> Lekin thaurayin ko Chouboli ka gusse se tamtamata hua chehra aur gusse mein uski nazo-adaa bohut bhayi thi. Woh agar mard hoti to woh yakeenan usse shaadi kar leti. Khair woh shaadi rachaane ko hee to wahan aayi thi. (40)
>
>> The *thakurayin* was very attracted to Chouboli's face glowing with anger and all her mannerisms drenched in rage. If she [the manager's daughter] were a man, she would have married Chouboli. Still it was, after all, to conduct a marriage that she had come there.

The manager's niece is intensely drawn to Chouboli, and the repeated implication is that Chouboli is similarly drawn to the *kissago*. This same-sex attraction is initially presented in the same manner as Olivia's love for Viola is in Shakespeare's *Twelfth Night*; in both texts the implication is that the older woman falls in love with the masculine femininity or feminine masculinity of the young boy she sees before her. Even though Olivia and Chouboli might be falling in love with a person presenting as a man, it is the inability to tell woman from man to which they seem really drawn. Thus, Olivia, after disallowing all amorous advances by men, seems to relent at her steward Malvolio's description of the latest emissary sent by her suitor Duke Orsino:

OLIVIA: Of what personage and years is he?

MALVOLIO: Not yet old enough for a man, nor young enough for a boy; as a squash is before 'tis a peascod, or a cooling when 'tis almost an apple: 'tis with him in standing water, between boy and man.

. . .

OLIVIA: Let him approach: call in my gentlewoman. (1.5.138–42; 145)

In a surprise turnaround, Olivia agrees to see Cesario, and indeed falls in love with her in short order. There is something in the description of Viola as being "between boy and man" that seems to have clinched the deal for Olivia. And what lies between a boy and man seems to be: a woman. Similarly, people try and dissuade the *thakurayin* from attempting to win Chouboli's hand by pointing to her youthfulness: "Tere to abhi dudh ke daant bhi nahin toote hain" [Your milk teeth haven't even fallen out yet], or "Jiski abhi masein bhi nahin bheegi hain, woh rajkumari se shaadi karne aaya hai" [He who is still wet behind the ears, whose facial hair has not yet sprouted, he has the temerity to try and marry the princess] (17).

This gendered indeterminacy seems attractive to women all over the literary world. In *Chouboli*, the formal insistence on breaking down borders of language and genre is echoed by a sharp questioning of the boundaries between the sexes and interrogating the laws as they have been laid down for desire:

Woh to khud aurat thi par uspar Chouboli ke husn ka nasha chadh raha tha; jab uski sachai saamne aayegi to na jaane shahzadi ka kya radde amal ho. Aur agar koi ummeedvar sach mein uska var jeet leta to—nahin, nahin, koi mard

iss kaabil nahin tha ki woh Chouboli ka haath jeet sakey, kissi mard se
haarne par usski aukat kam ho jaayegi, mardon ki to zaat hi bemurrawat hai,
unhe kya hak pohunchta hai ki woh uski barabri karein. Chouboli poori
aurat zaat ki numayinda thi, use surkhru hona hi tha. (53)

   She herself was a woman, but she found Chouboli's beauty intoxicating:
who knows how Chouboli will react when the manager's niece is revealed
to be a woman! And what if some hopeful man had indeed won Chouboli
in marriage—no, no, no man was worthy enough to win Chouboli's hand;
if she had lost to a man, then her status would have been lowered. The entire
race of men is selfish: what right did they have to try and match themselves
with Chouboli? The princess is the gem of the entire female race, so the
manager's niece had no choice but to win in her endeavor—her very being,
and that of womankind, depended on it.

There is here a curious mix of defiance—men are worthless—and conformity: How will Chouboli react to the knowledge that the *thakurayin* is
a woman? This passage both keeps men and women apart *and* ignores the
differences between them. The double movement is interesting because it
does not come down on the side either of conformity or defiance: it both
questions heterosexuality and adheres by its norms. But what is even more
interesting—and this is borne out also at the end of Chouboli's *dastan*—
is that despite the conservative view of seeing men and women as being
completely different species from one another, the manager's niece's love
for Chouboli exists in the text entirely without negative comment, and
even with a certain familiarity: homosexuality does not excite the invocation of difference. There is never any moral opprobrium attached to it,
nor does it necessitate any explanatory apparatus: Chouboli is beautiful,
and the manager's niece is deeply attracted to her beauty. The but-I-am-a-
woman comment that is wheeled out every now and then is done so by
the manager's niece herself, never by the narrative or by any other character in the story. And even the manager's niece, as we see, wheels it out only
to send it packing with great dispatch.

ACT IV: SEXUAL DIFFERENCE

Does this mean that *Chouboli* is a story of lesbian love? The narrative is set
in the framework of a heterosexual marriage (indeed, a series of them),
and Chouboli and the *thakur* end up as man and (third) wife. But Chouboli
also ends up with the second wife, the *thakurayin*, the manager's niece, the

kissago. She is linked with the force of the theatrical narrative, which is also the locus of its lesbian desire. In the *dastan*, though, Chouboli's relationship with the *thakurayin* is never described as a lesbian relation; there seems to be something in the *dastan* of Chouboli that asks us to jettison identitarian categories even and especially during the articulation of desire. Chouboli both is and is not a lesbian: she is attracted to the *kissago*, but her desire does not conform to a particularity. Instead, it is in the movement of narrative that both women find their desire: Chouboli in speaking four times in one night, and the manager's niece in telling her tales that prompt such speech. As the second performance of *Chouboli* made clear, *what* Chouboli says is secondary to the fact of her speaking. The *thakurayin* repeatedly announces that none of her riddles has a correct answer—the important thing is that they be addressed.[28] The narrative frisson between these two women, then, lies not in the truth value of what they say, but in the very movement of their tongues.

At the end of the *dastan*, when Chouboli and the *thakurayin* have to decide what to do with their relationship—they are, after all, husband and wife—they must take recourse to the stories that lie before them. At least three of the four tales that the manager's niece has narrated have at their heart the dilemma of desire. In one, a newlywed wife has to negotiate between an absent husband and a lascivious neighbor; in this tale the woman gives in to the neighbor but is then rejected after the neighbor inadvertently addresses her as his daughter. Sexual love is sublimated into filial love and the woman parts from her neighbor on good terms, and even tells her husband the truth about her straying desires (he is a traveler who too, we presume, has desires that wander). In another, Pygmalion-like tale, a woman is fashioned out of wood by a woodworker, clothed by a dressmaker, adorned by a jeweler, bangled by a bangle-maker, and given life by a priest, and then has to decide which one of them is her husband. Several answers are suggested, but each rouses Chouboli to further heights of fury until she answers that the wood-woman can only be married to the bangle-maker since the bestowal of bangles signifies marriage. After this arbitrary adjudication of desire comes yet another tale. In this one, provocatively titled "Who Is the Husband," a woman has to decide—*Cymbeline*-like—between the mismatched trunks and heads of her husband and his best friend. This last story is rather bizarre: "Ek ganv mein ek Rajput aur ek Jat saath-saath rehte the, dono gehre dost the, din raat chobeeson ghante kaya aur chhaya ki tarah saath-saath rehte the." [In a village a Rajput and a Jat were the best of friends, lived side-by-side, day and night, all twenty-four hours they were inseparable, joined together like a body and its shadow.] (61). Incensed at the way in which his in-laws have treated his friend, the Rajput enters a temple dedicated to Shiva and sacrifices his life in protest for the god not having honored his devotee's desire that his friend be treated well. When the Jat enters the temple to inquire after his friend, he sees him lying dead with his neck slit: "Usne aav dekha na taav aur ussi talwar ka ek waar apni gardan par kiya aur dost ke bagal mein gir padda. Jab dono dost zinda the to ek saath saans lete the, ab jab dono phaut ho gaye the to dono ka khoon aapas me mil kar beh raha tha, dono ek doosre ke khoon me vileen ho gaye." [Looking neither right nor left, the Jat picked up the same sword, cut off his neck, and fell dead by the side of his friend. When the two were alive, they would lie together, now that both were dead, their blood mingled together as it flowed. Each man dissolved in the other's blood.] (64). What seems clear is that by dissolving into one another the two men have achieved the union they seem to have fervently desired through life and death.

The Rajput's new bride enters the temple and is granted a favor by Parvati, Shiva's consort: she can rejoin the severed heads and bodies of her husband and his friend. In her nervousness the new bride attaches the wrong head to the wrong trunk and now faces a dilemma: "Dulhan ke samne ek ajeeb muamma aa khada hua tha—dono mein se uska pati kaun tha: Rajput ke ghad wala Jat sar tha ya Jaat ke ghad wala Rajput sar?" [The bride was now in an odd predicament: Which of the two was her husband? The one with the Rajput's body and the Jat's head, or the one with the Jat's body and the Rajput's head?] (65). The tale remains open-ended on what the bride will do. In a sense, of course, *what* she does is not important, nor whom she chooses (the text gives us justification for two different choices); what is important is that this tale gives us desires that communicate themselves in different guises, all of which complicate the relation between desires and bodies. And while the story itself may seem like a classic instance of a woman placed in the middle of a homo social/sexual relation, it is also a tale of complicating the particular identities that we attach to bodies and desires.

For *dastangoi*, these complications of desire are part of its generic fabric: one cannot know who is speaking as what and when, whose desires are being mouthed by whom, because that takes away from the suspense of the tale. For Badiou, such nonidentitarian desires are part of the very domain of the theater:

A major stake of theatre, already suspect to every church, consists in propos-
ing the following thesis: the two sexes differ radically, but there is nothing
substantial in this difference. Theatre introduces us, through its play, to this
first point of ethics: know that no difference is natural, beginning with the
difference that institutes that there are men and women. . . .

Theatre carries with it from the origin an essential "feminism" that is
based not on equality but on the substantial nothingness of that which
marks the difference of the sexes, the purely logical and transparent character of this marking. Or again, if you want, the woman does not exist, since a
man or a woman, actor or actress, is justified in producing its signs or its
in-sign-ia. (218)

In the theater, the difference between the sexes is insubstantial: it lacks
positive content. For Badiou, this is what we might call the essence of
indifference—differences are never essential, and "singularity is a composition without a concept" (221). The insubstantiality of the difference
between men and women does not mean that men and women do not
exist—evidently they do. But theater interrupts the seeming solidity of
that difference by showing it does not attach to prefabricated bodies: there
is no logical relation between a body and the desires that emanate from
or attach to it. Rephrasing Jacques Lacan's formulation about the nonexis-
tence of the sexual relation, Badiou suggests that "the woman" does not
exist substantially because she can be imitated at any point. And if "the
woman"—real or imitated—has long been taken by the Church and anti-
theatricalists in general as the exemplar of all that is wrong with the theater
because s/he undermines the distinction between the sexes, then perhaps
it is time to take that criticism seriously. In the theater, the refusal of fixity
is embodied by the *necessity* for the body to change its clothes, makeup,
mannerisms, and desires. Theatricality involves an incessant movement
between selves, and this movement in turn refuses a positive correlation
between bodies and identities. A theatrical body by definition cannot have
a defined set of desires.

This movement away from a fixed correlation between bodies and
desires is the hallmark of a strand of Urdu poetry called *rekhti*—so named
because it is the feminine version of *rekhta*, the common name for literary
Urdu. *Rekhti* does not name all genres of literary Urdu: rather, it is that
mode of poetry in which the narrative voice (regardless of the voice that
narrates it), and the vocabulary, is that of a woman. C. M. Naim elaborates:

It should be underscored here that it was not just having a female narrative voice that differentiated the rekhti from other genres, for that alone could be true of any number of ghazals written in Dakani that are now described as being in the "Indic" mode. (In fact, in many verses of Hashimi and Insha we can discern a male addressing a female.) Rather, the chief distinguishing feature was the so-called "feminine-ness" of its vocabulary and themes. That becomes clear from the definition set forth by Ahad Ali Khan Yakta, who finished his tazkira in 1834, not too long after Rangin and Insha had popularized the rekhti in Lucknow: "Rekhti is a kind of poetry in which only the speech and idioms of women are used and only those matters are mentioned that happen between women or between a woman and a man. Further, it must not contain any word or phrase that is exclusive to men." (7)[29]

Popularized by the poets Rangin and Insha in the eighteenth and nineteenth centuries, *rekhti* presumed a transvestite cast—this was poetry written primarily by men, but only about and in the voice of women.[30] The "language of women" was impersonated by poets who made themselves over into something surprising for the sake of their art, and even perhaps for the sake of their sexual pleasure. In writing *rekhti*, poets allowed form— poetry written in bastardized Urdu in a transvestite voice—to echo closely their content of transgressive desire. *Rekhti* has come in for criticism from scholars who consider its transvestism "merely" that of words, and have denounced it as a satiric form aimed at the degradation of women.[31] But what other scholars such as Ruth Vanita have pointed out is that the transvestism of *rekhti* lies not only in the fact that men speak in women's voices; it also persists in the fact that *rekhti* often speaks explicitly of lesbian desires and sexual encounters between women. *Rekhti* also makes clear that language is never a transparent indicator: not only do "men" speak like "women," but they all speak in a mixture of tongues that defies classification. Like the *dastan* of Chouboli, the Urdu of *rekhti* borrows freely from tropes belonging to Hindu devotional poetry, and "dr[aw] attention to th[e] 'impure' mingling that is the hallmark of [its] indigenous urbanity, distinct from the urbanity of a 'pure' Persianate provenance" (15).[32]

Like the Urdu language in general, only even more so, *rekhti* parades the badge of its insubstantiality: it is a form in which many traditions and cultures and languages mingle. Indeed, the unusual form and transgressive content of *rekhti* mark the emergence of an impure Hindustani poetics, or rather, of a Hindustani poetics of impurity. As opposed to an increasingly idealized Wordsworthian "naturalness," *rekhti* flaunted its artifice, including the artifice of a speaking voice presumed to be neither definitively male nor female. *Rekhti* poetry was transvestite both linguistically and sartorially as the male poets who composed and recited in the genre often also dressed up as women while performing at *mushairas*. As Vanita notes in relation to scholars who accuse *rekhti* of being just another conventional form of straight male release:

> Exclusively heterosexual or not, *Rekhti* poets and their audiences lived in a world where male homoerotic relations were prevalent, visible, and often celebrated in verse. To assume that their attitudes to all women and therefore to female homoeroticism could never have been anything but contemptuous seems to reflect not so much *Rekhti* itself as modern presumptions about pre-modern social arrangements. (47)[33]

The poetics of impurity that Urdu excelled in, and that was stamped out by the British colonial enterprise in the name of higher truths and utilitarianism, was equally a poetics of linguistic and sexual miscegenation. *Rekhti*, like the *ghazal*, and like *dastangoi*, revels in linguistic mixtures, porous boundaries, and mobile desires. And even though *rekhti* names a distinct genre of Urdu poetry, *dastangoi* is marked by many of the same features. In terms of narrative, *Chouboli* frequently speaks in a woman's voice, while in terms of form, the *dastan* uses a transvestite language including Urdu, Hindi, Rajasthani, and English. It contains language from the woman's sphere and is narrated by a male *dastango* who takes on this woman's language. Most important, *dastangoi*, like *rekhti*, insists on the mobility of desire, and on its indifference to bodily truth. Men speak as women—both the *dastangos* of *Chouboli*, Mahmood Farooqui and Danish Husain, took turns to speak the woman's part in the *dastan*, and did not change the tenor of their voice in order to do so—and women dress as men. In the tale, even when women stop dressing as men, they do not stop desiring women. In the telling of the tale, there were two men on stage mimetically related to the woman in the *dastan* who dresses as a man, thus throwing their own ontological status into question. In *Chouboli*, the desires of women and men are indifferently related to what we like to think of as their identity.

This break in the seeming solidity of bodily identity is induced by the fracture of mimesis and marks what Badiou terms the "feminism" of the theater:

If the theatre text is such that only the exception of a representation gives it existence, if qua theatre text it is subject, for its properly theatrical totalization, to the singular point of the instant of the play that itself is outside of the text being played, then we can legitimately say that theatre writes itself "not-all," as opposed to the compact and self-sufficient world that is the imaginary of the classical novel. It follows that the theatre, perpetually subject to the spectacular vanishing of its being, belongs in effect to the feminine sphere. It, too, is the irony of community. We know, moreover, that by way of transvestism, through sexual insecurity, by the farcical auctioning up of the phallus, theatre posts this latent derision of the glorious "All" of masculinity. This clarifies why the churches have a tendency to put actors, theatre, and women in the same obscure bag. (212–13)

Theater champions an anti-ontology in which being can never coincide with itself. The theater text is not the same as its enacted representation, the enacted representation in turn is not reducible to the actors' ontology, and neither is the same from show to show or day to day. "Perpetually subject to the spectacular vanishing of its being," the theater is witness to, indeed necessitates, the insubstantiality of identity. There is never coincidence among the many elements of the theatrical self or of the theater itself. If we enter the theater understanding "being" as the particularity we attach to a body, then the theater cannot tolerate such a particular. Instead, it unmoors bodies—fleshly and textual—from trajectories of specificity and opens them up to interpretation. The feminism of the theater rests in this incompletion: theater's desire to be closed is tempered by its insistence on what Badiou, along with Naim, calls its transvestism. By allowing the phallus to be a prop, the theater shows up the All as being not-all-that and not-all-there. The question it poses, then, is whether or not the audience can retain its hold on a self when the spectacle it has paid to watch insists on the impossibility of that self. Can we go to the theater and continue to have a self that owns its desire?

It is this question that animates *Chouboli*: Does particularity explain desire, or can women and men have desires not confined to bodily identities? Can we be certain who is and who is not a man or a woman, and do our desires follow suit? What difference does it make to the audience when a narrative thread presents two women in love rather than a recognizably heterosexual love story? Does the former have the power to fight homophobia, or can it be even more radical than that? Can *Chouboli*, for instance, open us up to questioning the fundamental categories of gender and sexuality within which we narrate ourselves instead of merely providing an anodyne "acceptance" of lesbian love? Can *Chouboli* teach us to be indifferent to (our) identity?

At the end of Chouboli's *dastan*, the *thakur* and Chouboli are presented publicly as a heterosexual couple. This is not because heterosexuality has suddenly trumped all other erotic energies in the tale, as can formally so often be the case at the end of Shakespeare plays. Rather, since the *thakur* is the one who had set off to win Chouboli's hand, it might have seemed odd if his wife were the one to have come back with the prize; this is entirely a narrative dilemma and not a moral or sexual one. And neither is the heterosexual coupling of Chouboli and the *thakur* the actual end of the *dastan*. Chouboli chafes at the thought of having to be the *thakur*'s wife, calling him a fool and a worthless idiot not deserving of her wit and beauty; she positively revels in the fact that "koi mard mujhe nahin haraa paaya; agar koi mujhse paar paaya to woh ek aurat hee thi" [no man has been able to defeat me; if I have been vanquished by anyone, then that person is a woman] (68). But the manager's niece prevails, and says she will first humiliate the *thakur*, and then make him give up his bad habit of archery. "[P]hir hum usse ek kavvhakaun banaa ke apne saath rakh lenge, woh hamari rakhwali karega" [Then we will keep him by our side like a scarecrow so he can provide us with some security] (70). This scarecrow figure—pathetic, straw-colored, with the phallus-as-a-prop—is what heterosexuality is reduced to in this *dastan*; the lesbians get to giggle behind doors and supply the *thakur* with their wisdom so he can administer his realm better than he has in the past. Unlike even the most daring Shakespearean comedies (*A Midsummer Night's Dream* or *Twelfth Night*) that inevitably end with the dance of heterosexuality, *Chouboli* refuses to give up on its homoerotic attachments. In this tale, lesbians rule. The End.

Except the question still remains about whether or not they are lesbians. The *dastan* of *Chouboli* seems uninterested in the particulars of its characters' sexual and domestic arrangements even as it gives us an engrossing love story between two witty and beautiful women. This lack of particularity has resulted in the fact that no scholar adduces *Chouboli* as an example of a lesbian story. When researchers want to find "lesbianism" in Detha's oeuvre, they turn to *Dohri Zindagi* (Two Lives), a short story about two women who get married to one another, briefly transform into a heterosexual couple, and then run away screaming from heterosexuality to re-embrace their lesbian marriage. Unlike in *Dohri Zindagi*, there are no markers in *Chouboli* about the two women's sexual specificity: they are two women in love with one another, but they are also married to the same man. Indeed, we are told early on in the text that the *thakurayin*, unlike Chouboli, had no objection to marrying the *thakur*, despite his obnoxious archery habit. Lest we conclude from this that the *thakurayin* is "really" bisexual, however, it might be best to consider what we lose by arriving at conclusions about identity. At the level of narrative, if the women end up as lesbians, then what do we say about their beginning? If they are bisexual, then where is the surprise about their falling in love with one another? If they are heterosexual, then how do they end up together at all? No matter what the identity at which we arrive, Chouboli and the *thakurayin*'s desires have shifted from what we might have thought them to be, and do not settle. *Chouboli* allows its women to be all these identities at once without fitting them into any single position. It does not legislate the identitarian boundaries among lesbianism, bisexuality, and heterosexuality. The women can be all of the above without calling themselves any one; what is most important in the *dastan* is that like the language in which the story is narrated, their desires are mobile and travel at will without needing an identitarian explanatory apparatus to contain them. Far from trying to make lesbianism palatable to what might inevitably be an unthinking or even actively homophobic audience, then, *Chouboli* refuses to identify its characters' desires. Or rather, it refuses to correlate their desires to an identity.

Perhaps because of this refusal, Mahmood Farooqui added two names to his version of Merrill's translation of Detha's scripted oral tale, both from the *rekhti* tradition. Chouboli and the *kissago* call one another "sakhi" and "guiyan" while debating what to do with the *thakur* at the end of the *dastan*. Both these terms clearly indicate that the two women are in a sexual and/or romantic relationship with one another. Despite this addition, however, not a single member of the audience I spoke to after the two performances registered the *dastan* as a tale of lesbian love. Not a single one of the reviews picked up on this either.[34] Even those who spoke of the syncretic language of the *dastan* failed to note the sexual echoes of that syncretism in the tale.

Maybe this is because general audiences are so hetero-centric that *Chouboli*'s tale of erotic attachment between two women pales into insignificance in light of the partly heterosexual ending. But, depending on the

audience, *Chouboli* could equally have been celebrated as a *dastan* of lesbian love and its heterosexuality completely ignored. Whether the particular verdict about the tale is hetero or homo, then, what is more interesting
to contemplate is that most audiences simply do not want to undertake the
difficult task of *unthinking* particularity—in Badiou's words, "Who would
not detest the fact of having paid for pleasure and being forced to perform a kind of work?"—and so sexual identity of any kind becomes, yet
again, the default mode into which the tale gets slotted. Indeed, it is easier
to think of the *dastan* in terms of identity than it is to think of it as undoing
identity altogether. Yet the *dastan* of Chouboli moves itself and us out of
categories of particularity. This is what makes *Chouboli* an event.

ACT V: INDIFFERENCE

For Badiou, an event is that which disallows modes of particularity by
refusing to abide by the categories we already know. The ability to let go
of the differences that define us and others, the ability to withhold a correspondence between self and identity, is what marks an event. It necessitates the embrace of an indifference that does not continue to cling to
the differences within which we live. This indifference is not skepticism
so much as the ability to think anti-ontologically. It refuses to base itself in
identitarian categories, preferring instead to interrupt the line that all-too-
easily connects bodies with identities, affiliations, and desires.

I have termed this indifference "universal" because it points to a failure
of identity that cuts across boundaries. And I have argued that this failure
is "queer" because it takes into account the surprising effects of desire. In
Chouboli, for instance, the universal failure of desire to correspond to identity is what makes it queer: the *thakurayin*, the *kissago*, the manager's niece
are all the same person, but also not. S/he desires different people and different desiring configurations but never settles for only one: s/he lives in
difference but embodies indifference. Similarly, the text is in Urdu, Hindi,
Rajasthani, English—all and none at once. In this *dastan*, identity dissolves
in the face of desire, and desire no longer gives us a face with which to
identify it.

This is the primary reason why *dastangoi* seems to offer the performative equivalent of a queer universalism: its form and content both propose
multiplicities but refuse to resolve into any one. This theatricalized narrative acts out all that is evental about the theater, but it also goes beyond
those parameters. After all, *dastangoi* is a narrative performance rather than

an enacted one: it is an oral fantasy with no props, acts, or movement. When it narrates its superabundance of desire, it does so on and in a body that does not change its clothes or its voice to signal a gendered and sexual change in the narrative. Male *dastangos* play men and women and supernatural elements and inanimate objects interchangeably and do not go offstage in order to change the scene. They are always present, always audible, always visible, and they are always indifferent to their identities. If, as the epigraph to this chapter suggests, "Theatre makes it known to you that you will not be able innocently to remain *in your place*," then *dastangoi* produces that wrenching action more effectively even than "normal" theater, and it does so by not moving at all. The *dastan* soars with inventive tales and magical language, it dives into realms unseen and unknown, it produces effects of which the cinema can only dream. And it does all this by being indifferent to difference; by taking desire seriously enough not to pigeonhole it into identity. *Chouboli* theorizes a queer universalism by insisting that indifference to difference pays difference the most respect by not paying it too much heed. Might we say, then, that queer theory is moving now to where the *dastan* once was?

While theorizing the unconscious, Sigmund Freud suggested that "Wo es war, soll ich werden"—Where id was, there ego shall be.[35] This suggests that the formation of the ego—what we call the self, our identity—will perforce elbow out and supersede the id's domain of unregulated desire. This is an impossible task, as Freud himself goes on to add, but it is necessary to *pretend* as though it is possible if we want to be accepted as social animals. In our current social and theoretical idiolects, this desire for acceptance has so trumped the swoops of desire that identitarian particularity has increasingly disowned desire's superabundance. We cling to identity and take offense at desire. But *dastangoi* and queer theory both suggest that this supersession is impossible. The id in id-entity insists that the entity we like to call a self is always haunted by the id, always shaped and unshaped by it: our desires cannot be contained by us; we are undone by desire.

Chouboli presents the id in all its eruptions and does not attempt to assert the supremacy of the entity. There is no desire for unity, only fragments that cannot be shored up against the ruin of the self. The *dastan*'s language wanders, as do its desires, and it names neither one with certainty. Even the very name of Urdu, as we have seen, refuses to settle on any single dialect, in much the same way as the *thakurayin* does not settle in any one desiring arrangement. For Pritchett, "Western literary criticism

has generally embraced visions of literature much closer to the autonomous, intertextual 'game of words'" (168) that marks Urdu poetry (for
her, specifically, the *ghazal*) than it has the reforming vision of a "natural"
poetry leached of desire. In such an understanding, literary theory *is* Urdu
poetry. And queer theory too, since Urdu poetry revels in the surprises
rather than the identities that desire generates. But this does not mean
that Urdu poetry is the "precursor" of Western literary theory or that it is
the oriental equivalent of the occidental academy—this is not an exercise
in correcting chronology and identifying progenitors. Rather, the theoretical lessons of *dastangoi* suggest a form of universalism that both the
Urdu poets and queer theory embrace across time and space. In Pritchett's
words:

> Our own generation can take pride in a widening range of cultural encoun-
> ters that has opened over time to more and more people. We expect cultures
> to clash, and we try to appreciate the dissonances. But we also know that (as
> Azad put it) "if you examine the temperaments of individual men who live
> thousands of miles apart and in countries with different characters, you will
> see, since human nature is one, to what extent their thoughts resemble each
> other's." (xvii)

Whether or not we agree that human nature is one, what is astonishing is
a nineteenth-century Urdu poet's sense of a universal connection that particularism has since significantly eroded. Despite what might be taken at
first glance as an Enlightenment version of universalism, Azad's mantra
does not indicate hierarchies among people or positions (when the time
came to do that, he put Urdu poetry below that of Wordsworth). Instead,
it suggests an indifference to differences of geography and culture, an investment in intellectual and desiring energies that can speak across identitarian boundaries. Like *Chouboli*'s lesbians, Azad's poetics encourage us
to travel without penalty. Indeed, all the characters in this *dastan*—from
Chouboli to the *kissago*, from Badiou to the theater, from Urdu poetry to
dastangoi, from Shakespeare to Shonibare—desire, write, and enact, indifference. Bringing together Shakespeare and Chouboli, Badiou and Freud,
the *kissago* and Pritchett, darkness and the stage, postcolonial desire and
unanchored bodies, indifference refuses to let us become entrenched in our
identity positions. It even allows us to be touched—perhaps four times in
one night—by the tongue of desire.

Coda

Queer and Universal

The burning question in relation to queer theory is whether or not its capaciousness has gone "too far." Does queerness have a specificity that can be grounded in particular bodies and practices? Or is everything (and therefore nothing?) queer? Another way of asking this question is if queerness is a particular or a universal. Is it bounded by and to an essence or does it allow us to vacate ontology? What do we mean if we say that queerness vacates ontology? And how can we even speak of queerness if there is no spandex within which it can take shape? These questions all presume a friction about the nature and ethics of queerness. If it is a thing, then to whom or what does it belong? What is the *particularity* of queerness?

Let us take, for instance, the partition of India and Pakistan in 1947, which pitted against one another entities that had for centuries shared lands, languages, and cultures. This partition has the advantage of not being considered typical fare for queer theorization; in other words, it seems explicitly to be outside the ambit of queerness, suggesting in fact that not everything is queer. But it also has the advantage of theorizing the relation between the particular and the universal, which is the subject of this book's queer speculations. The partition of India and Pakistan assumed the separation of poetic desires, sexual longings, quotidian cooking, and diverse religions that had extended across both sides of the border. Even more, it assumed that these newly separated particulars justified the formation of new states. Suddenly, and in strange twists, the two strands of a double helix were forced apart with great violence, and each strand proclaimed itself as an *identity* that was oppositionally supreme over the other. From both sides, this identitarian violence was directed not just externally toward a putative enemy, but also internally toward the sexual politics of a religion notoriously impossible to pin down. In the lead-up to and aftermath of 1947, Hinduism was equated with chasteness and non-Western sexuality, while Islam was described as the province of homosexuality and pederasty. But equally, Hinduism was considered the domain of the luxuriant sensuality of the *Kama Sutra*, while Islam was cast as the strict religion that shunned Western sexualities (including homosexuality). So Islam was both strict and decadent, while Hindusim was both perverted and chaste. Neither religion can be unwrinkled, let alone made consistent, yet each was cast in 1947 as supporting the identity of an entire nation and people. The two religions needed to be distinguished—once and for all, fundamentally—from each other in order to provide the basis for the partition of India and Pakistan. But how can one, let alone two, nations be founded on the basis of religions that are allocated characteristics so arbitrarily?[1]

In such cases, partition is the name for imposing coherence on chaos and foisting identity on particularity. This investment in ontological coherence comes at a cost, however. Most immediately, that cost can be seen in the violence that religiously motivated geopolitical partitions—Eire/Ulster, Pakistan/India, Israel/Palestine—have spawned.[2] The politics of particularity that undergirds these partitions assumes—violently—that an ontological wholeness can be assigned to a (religious) particular. Such a politics—as exemplified by the partition of India and Pakistan—not only encourages arbitrary partitions but then insists that these partitions be converted into natural identities that halt desire at the border. It insists that a particular is more important than a universal. This movement from particular to identitarian is a peculiar one because it assigns wholeness to a part and assumes identity over what is only arbitrary. Partitions are never full, but they thrive on the illusion of fullness.

It is in the sense of being translated from a part to a whole that partition becomes cognate with particularity. The particular—what the *OED* defines as "[b]elonging to or affecting only a part of something; partial; not universal"—gives us a predicate on the basis of which a thing is allowed to be a thing; a particular permits a being to be ontologically recognizable with reference to that particular. So, for instance, blackness is a particular, as is homosexuality, femininity, baldness, and so on. Particularity, like partition, assumes metonymically that a part can stand as and for a whole. In doing so, particularity forgets its own fragmentariness in favor of identity; it takes on the mantle of wholeness by ignoring the theoretical insight that would see the whole punningly as a hole, bereft of integrity rather than filled with plenitude. Particulars are universal—we all have them. Indeed, "we" wouldn't be ourselves if we didn't have a set of particulars by which to be identified. But it is a far cry from having particulars to imagining them as identities. And it is a giant leap to assume that *having* something in common makes identitarian comrades of us all. In such a particularist argument, queerness is an attribute that is owned by specific people.

Universalism, in contradistinction, does not describe the condition in which everyone *has* the same thing. Rather, universalism in the sense I am using it in this book is not tantamount to wholeness—to the "insistent teleological imperatives and future-oriented acts" that Lee Edelman has described as politics' pretext.[3] Instead, what is universal is the ontological impossibility of the self-identical part. Any reconsideration of the politics of partition will thus have to reconsider the regime of the particular. Being governed by identitarian particularity ceaselessly creates the part *as* the whole. An alternative to this regime would challenge the particular as the basis on which people, desires, ideas, and countries get divided. In this alternative politics to the reign of the particular, universalism peddles what we may term partitions in all, refusing to make difference coherent, self-identical, or the basis for identity. Even as it acknowledges that differences abound, universalism does not gather them together as the foundation for partition. Instead, universalism is the realm in which the fact of social, cultural, religious, and sexual difference does not take away from the reality that we are all different even from our "own" differences. As Alain Badiou suggests, "The universal is not the negation of particularity. It is the measured advance across a distance relative to *perpetually* subsisting particularity" (emphasis mine). Particulars exist *and* they cannot be translated into ontological identities. Universalism is a movement across partitions that does not privilege any one particular as a basis for ontology. Instead, it allows us to universalize partition as the condition within which we all labor.

Equally, universalism does not consist in *un*doing partition; it does not propose an opposite action with which to counter in Newtonian fashion the force of the partitive. Indeed, undoing partition would suggest a belief in an originary whole from which we have declined. This is the biblical view of the world as it is the view of Plato's Aristophanes on love. But a universalist understanding of partition, far from suggesting that partition can be undone, insists instead that it can never in fact be full. Partition does not and cannot part, just as it does not and cannot fill. Indeed, universalizing the particular as paradoxically being nonontological can shock us out of our current ways of thinking about ontology and epistemology. A partition that suggests absolute oppositional difference between particulars also reveals a universal that never belongs. People continually wander between states of emotion and being and politics; the migratory flow across sexual borders as much as geographical ones gives the lie to ontological identities based on particularities. If a universal names not an attribute that can be owned by a particular group but rather a characteristic that marks all political beings, then the condition of being unwholesomely partitioned is universal. Universalism militates against an identity politics in which inhabiting a particularity defines our place in the world. Instead, it insists on straddling, on standing athwart, ontological categories that divide up the world and the people in it. Shunning politics' desire to be absolute, universalism points out instead the "structural antagonism" that denies wholeness to particularity; it fractures the notion that particularity can be the basis of a nation-state or even just of a state of being.

But even if partition has succeeded in climbing up on the back of universalism, then we must remember that its success is only relatively recent and by no means complete. The current triumph of partitioned particularity is Universalist in the Enlightenment sense of the term—it is one difference pretending to be absolute. Indeed, it believes completely that the idea of identitarian difference itself is universal.[4] Such a notion of universalism is entirely compatible with our current obsession with particularity, since both assume that a particular can be made into an ontological whole. However, universalism in the Badiousian sense focuses on the inability of any particularity to ascend to the level of a universal. Instead, universalism names the impossibility of having any particular assume ontological wholeness. Even at a glance, there is not a single aspect of our lived lives that conforms to the strictures of particularist identity: Men act like women, women behave like men; skin color undergoes changes of perception; facial features get rearranged; religions get converted; languages are acquired and lost; boundaries of nation-states are transgressed, and global finance makes paupers of us all. Even as politics might base itself in ontological absolutes, the *lived reality* of our lives is that we are not ontologically grounded. Such a lack of grounding repeatedly, universally, undermines the attempt to forge an ontology out of a particular. Keeping open the question of whether or not the self can ever coincide with itself, universalism is the language for all because it is the language of the not-all. Indeed, for Alain Badiou, universalism tears through knowability because it irrevocably shifts the protocols by which we know and on the basis of which we create epistmologies: "There is no acceptable ontological matrix of the [universal]" (190).[5]

Such a universalism militates against owning an ontological particular. It cannot ground queer theory in sexual identity even as it can highlight the queerness in not cleaving to particularity. As such, what's queer about queer theory is its ability to recognize and sympathize with longings across borders, to refuse the logic of particularity in relation to desire; to keep the door universally open rather than shutting it behind our backs; to think of desire as that which moves across rather than being confined to sexual acts and identities.

A theory that would undermine this ontology by dwelling incessantly on the idea of noncohering particulars would be both queer and universal—queer because universal. Such an argument might at first seem counterintuitive. How can something universal also be queer, given our current understanding of queer as the thing that runs aslant of the normative and our long-standing association with the universal as something normative? But if we consider that queerness—at a minimum—refuses the predeterminable cohesion of identity, then we are immediately in the domain of the universal. If we accept further that queerness resists the regime of identitarian truth, then we can theorize a universalism that is in significant ways different from the Hegelian notion of the perfection of the German State. Universalism as the political *thing* that makes particulars fail to cohere; universalism as the idea that spurs longing across borders; universalism as the notion that allows intellectual ferment: these are the domains of the queer. The universalism of noncohering particulars is queer, then, because it shows up the futility of using partition as a bulwark against the migration of peoples, ideas, and desires. A queer universalism does not belong anywhere, and it is owned by no one.

Notes

INTRODUCTION

1. Julian Murphet, "Cultural Studies and Alain Badiou," in *New Cultural Studies: Adventures in Theory,* ed. Claire Birchall and Gary Hall (Athens: University of Georgia Press, 2007), 147–60.

2. David Theo Goldberg, ed., *Multiculturalism: A Critical Reader* (Hoboken, N.J.: Wiley Blackwell, 2009).

3. Terence Turner, "Anthropology and Multiculturalism: What Is Anthropology That Multiculturalists Should Be Mindful of It?" in *Multiculturalism: A Critical Reader,* 406–25, esp. 413.

4. The relation between bond and bondage is Goldberg's formulation. While describing the rise and forms of multiculturalism in the U.S. Academy, Goldberg states: "This conception [of an affirmative conception of identity], however, can cut both ways. The bond, as Michael Dyson illustrates, can also be a bondage; the tie is something that may hold one in" (*Multiculturalism,* 12).

5. Satya P. Mohanty, Paula M. L. Moya, Linda Martín Alcoff, and Michael Hames-García, eds., *Identity Politics Reconsidered (Future of Minority Studies)* (New York: Palgrave Macmillan), 2005.

6. All references to Shakespeare are to *The Norton Shakespeare* based on the Oxford Edition, ed. Stephen Greenblatt et al. (New York: W. W. Norton, 1997).

7. See, for instance, *Discipline and Punish,* especially the chapter on the Panopticon, and *Madness and Reason,* among others.

8. For more details, see my article on the case. http://www.asianage.com/columnists/presumption-penis-527. And also: http://www.hindustantimes.com/India-news/Kolkata/Police-say-Pramanik-is-male-doctors-contest-claim/Article1-958716.aspx.

9. See Frantz Fanon, *Black Skin, White Masks,* trans. Charles Lam Markmann (New York: Grove Press, 1967), esp. 145–51.

10. Judith Butler, Ernesto Laclau, and Slavoj Žižek, *Contingency, Hegemony, Universality: Contemporary Dialogues on the Left* (New York: Verso, 2000).

11. Alain Badiou, *Saint Paul: The Foundation of Universalism*, trans. Ray Brassier (Stanford: Stanford University Press, 2003).

12. Eric Lott, "After Identity, Politics: The Return of Universalism," *New Literary History* 31, no. 4 (Autumn 2000): 665–78.

13. Ernesto Laclau, *Emancipations* (New York: Verso, 1996).

14. There is also a suspicion that this very idea of "emptiness" is illusory. And so Butler suggests that "the particular and substantive claims about universality will finally take place under yet another rubric of universality, one which is radically empty, irreducible to specific content, signifying nothing other than the ongoing debate over its possible meanings. But is such a notion of universality ever as empty as it is posited to be? Or is there a specific form of universality which lays claim to being 'empty'" (*Contingency,* 167)? And Žižek adds that "the question is not just which particular content will hegemonize the empty place of universality—the question is, also and above all, which secret privileging and inclusions/exclusions had to occur for this empty place as such to emerge in the first place" (*Contingency,* 320). Fearing that the emptiness of universality merely glosses over a power struggle in which the powerful will, once again, emerge as the ones in power, both Butler and Žižek are wary of the alleged emptiness of universality. And indeed, Enlightenment claims for universality were filled with power that went unremarked as such.

15. G. W. F. Hegel, *Elements of the Philosophy of Right*, trans. H. B. Nisbet (Cambridge: Cambridge University Press, 2012), 38.

16. "The German Ideology," in *The Marx-Engels Reader*, 2nd ed., ed. Robert C. Tucker (New York: W. W. Norton, 1978), 192.

17. http://en.wikiquote.org/wiki/Subcomandante_Marcos.

18. Badiou's writing on desire is too inconsistent, at times too conservative, and at times too indebted to Lacanian psychoanalysis, for me to engage fully in this project. For a critique of Badiou's relation to a queer desire, see Lee Edelman's forthcoming book, *Bad Education*. Even though Badiou insists that "what is at issue [in the conceptualization of universalism] is desire" (79), he does little to exfoliate this statement, and certainly not in relation to the notions of queerness that I tease out here.

19. Jacques Lacan has described desire similarly as "paradoxical, erratic, eccentric, even scandalous." See "The Signification of the Phallus," in *Écrits,* trans. Bruce Fink (New York: W. W. Norton, 2007), 575–84; 579; Badiou's term for it is a "superabundance [that] cannot be assigned to any Whole" (78); for him, desire fully marks Paul's universalist project from over two thousand years ago.

20. But, one could argue, the very idea of a nonontologically determinable identity is a particular to which I am tethering universalism. Inasmuch as it seeks to populate the category of the universal, I must plead guilty to such a charge. But inasmuch as it refuses an ontological grounding, and therefore an identity, for itself, I must insist again that while queerness might be a particular idea, it is not a particular identity, and that difference is significant.

21. In *Cruel Optimism*, Lauren Berlant describes desire as a "desire to desubjectivize queerness" (Durham: Duke University Press, 2011), 18.

22. In *Queer Phenomenology: Orientations, Objects, Others* (Durham: Duke University Press, 2006), Sara Ahmed argues that the "word 'queer'... itself 'twists'... allow[ing] us to move between sexual and social registers, without flattening them or reducing them to a single line. Although this approach risks losing the specificity of queer as a commitment to a life of sexual deviation, it also sustains the significance of 'deviation' in what makes queer lives queer" (161).

23. Eve Kosofsky Sedgwick, *Epistemology of the Closet* (Berkeley: University of California Press, 1990), 85. Jonathan Goldberg, *Strangers on a Train* (Vancouver: Arsenal Pulp Press, 2012). While discussing Alfred Hitchcock's film in this Queer Film Classic, Goldberg quotes Eric Rohmer and Claude Chabrol's 1979 study of Hitchcock in which they note that "the seductive Uncle Charlie [in *Shadow of a Doubt*] will have as his cousins the Brandon of *Rope* and the Bruno Anthony of *Strangers on a Train*" (73). Goldberg then adds: "Far beyond the narrow confines of an invidious homosexual triptych, if still in terms we may deplore, Rohmer and Chabrol open Hitchcock's work to a homosexuality without limits. Rather than a world of persecuted gays, Hitchcock would seem instead to offer queer films, displaying not so much a minoritarian logic as a queer universalism (to recall again the categories developed by Sedgwick). It's here, I think, that we can take our pleasure in Hitchcock."

24. Ahmed further argues that we can "think about how queer politics might *involve* disorientation, without legislating disorientation as a politics. It is not that disorientation is always radical" (158).

25. For instance, if we say queerness is nonheterosexual, then we cannot account for closeted homos. If we say that queers are radical thinkers, then we cannot exclude fascists from its realm. These impossible exclusions raise the problem of not only how to define queerness positively in the sense of being filled with content, but also positively in terms of things that we like. As Ahmed suggests, "It is important... that we avoid assuming that 'deviation' is always on 'the side' of the progressive" (174). Queerness is neither a thing that can be affirmed nor a thing in the affirmative. Indeed, we might think of queerness as a paradigmatic instance of what it means for a seeming difference not to produce an ontology. Queerness cannot formulate its constituents; it points to the impossibility of fullness and coherence; it practices an indifference to particularity.

26. The relation between universalism and desire is not the same as the one between universalism and sexuality, the latter of which both Butler and Žižek have repeatedly discussed. Sexuality presumes an identity, which desire does not. Instead, desire—that allegedly transhistorical, universalizing term—insists on the fact that its object is not fixable or, finally, knowable. Further, any object that "fulfills" desire also leads to its death.

27. http://www.egs.edu/faculty/alain-badiou/articles/on-the-truth-process/.

28. This dictum from "The Eighteenth Brumaire of Louis Bonaparte" is rendered differently in different translations. In the classic *Marx-Engels Reader*, 2nd ed. (New York: W. W. Norton, 1978), Robert C. Tucker translates it as follows: "Men make their own history, but they do not make it just as they please; they do not make it under circumstances chosen by themselves, but under circumstances directly found, given and transmitted from the past" (595).

29. It is interesting to remember that one of the ways in which "will" was understood in the Renaissance was as a synonym for "desire."

30. Had my immigration officer been indifferent to my identity, then he might have waited and wanted to be *surprised* by my response. But surprise is, specifically, not the domain of the law, since we are all allegedly *equal* under it.

1. OUT OF AFRICA

1. "Setting the Stage," Yinka Shonibare MBE in Conversation with Anthony Downey, Catalogue Copy (New York: Prestel Verlag, 2008), 38–45, 42.

2. Nancy Hynes and John Picton, "Yinka Shonibare," *African Arts* 34, no. 3 (Autumn 2001): 60–73 and 93–95, 65.

3. Janet A. Kaplan et al., "Give & Take Conversations," an interview with Yinka Shonibare, *Art Journal* 61, no. 2 (Summer 2002): 68–91, 83.

4. http://www.zeleza.com/blogging/popular-culture/decapitating-colonialism -yinka-shonibare-new-york.

5. For a recent, detailed, and fascinating inquiry into Shonibare's encounter with Wilde, see Robert Stilling, "An Image of Europe: Yinka Shonibare's Postcolonial Decadence" (*PMLA* 128, no. 2 [March 2013]: 299–321). Stilling brings together postcolonial and aesthetic theory with suggestive implications for queer theory: "Shonibare's work suggests that this will to artifice may be more desirable for the contemporary postcolonial subject than any effort to establish stricter principles of historical realism would be" (310). Although Stilling does not speak about indifference, it is noteworthy that the essay's first quotation from Wilde is about how art is "absolutely indifferent to fact" (299).

6. http://www.oed.com.proxyau.wrlc.org/view/Entry/40748.

7. http://africa.si.edu/exhibits/shonibare/gallantry.html.

8. Georg Lukács, *The Theory of the Novel* (Boston: MIT Press, 1974), 41. But while Lukács uses the phrase to suggest that the novel attempts to feel at home everywhere, I see Shonibare's art embracing the idea that home is nowhere; it is as elusive as desire.

9. Hynes and Picton, "Yinka Shonibare," 62; emphasis mine.

10. Robert Hobbs, "Yinka Shonibare MBE: The Politics of Representation," Catalogue copy (New York: Prestel Verlag, 2008), 34.

11. Some of these ads can be viewed at http://www.youtube.com/watch?v=ALWw K7Vz4gY.

12. Badiou, *Saint Paul*, 11.

13. See Gilles Deleuze and Félix Guattari, *Kafka: Towards a Minor Literature,* Theory and History of Literature 30, trans. Dana Polan (Minneapolis: University of Minnesota Press, 1986).

14. See Michel Foucault, "The Repressive Hypothesis," in *The History of Sexuality*, vol. 1, trans. Robert Hurley (New York: Vintage, 1990).

15. Hynes and Picton, "Yinka Shonibare," 65.

16. Quoted in Crystal Bartolovich, "Figuring the (In)visible in an Imperial Weltstadt: The Case of Benjamin's Moor," *Cultural Critique* 52, Everyday Life (Autumn 2002): 167–208, 196.

17. Ibid., 197.

18. Ibid., 169.

19. Quoted in Norman L. Kleeblatt, "Identity Roller-Coaster," *Art Journal* 64, no. 1 (Spring 2005): 61–63.

20. "Setting the Stage," interview with Anthony Downey, 42.

21. Badiou, *Saint Paul*, 78.

22. Hobbs, "Yinka Shonibare MBE," 33–34.

23. The full text of the short story can be found at this site: http://search.proquest.com.proxyau.wrlc.org/docview/421786377/13907C74ADE1391FCE5/12?accountid=8285.

24. For details of a theatrical adaptation of Berger's short story at the Frick Museum in Pittsburgh, see Rick Kemp and Brian Jones, "The Museum of Desire: Cognition in Performance and Reception," *International Journal of the Arts in Society* 4, no. 5 (2010): 61–70.

25. Lacan, "The Signification of the Phallus," 575–84.

26. Orhan Pamuk, *The Museum of Innocence*, trans. Maureen Freely (New York: Alfred A. Knopf, 2010).

27. http://www.guardian.co.uk/artanddesign/2012/apr/20/orhan-pamuk-make-museums-much-smaller.

28. http://www.thedailybeast.com/newsweek/2012/08/26/orhan-pamuk-on-his-museum-of-innocence-in-istanbul.html.

29. Jacques Lacan, "Agency of the Letter in the Unconscious," in *Écrits: A Selection*, trans. Alan Sheridan (New York: W. W. Norton, 1977), 167.

30. Photo from http://observatory.designobserver.com/feature/the-museum-of-communicating-objects/36588/.

31. http://www.lacan.com/zizphilosophy3.htm.

32. http://www.thedailybeast.com/newsweek/2012/08/26/orhan-pamuk-on-his-museum-of-innocence-in-istanbul.html. In the same article, Pamuk goes on to outline a new field of study: "And finally, while browsing the flea markets of non-Western cities (Bombay, Buenos Aires, St. Petersburg) in the 2000s, I realized that exactly the same old saltshakers, clocks, and sundry knickknacks that I saw in increasingly wealthy Istanbul's junk shops were in fact easily found the world over. Like migratory birds,

objects too traveled on mysterious flyways. Perhaps we need a new field of study—
'Comparative Modernity'?—to develop and put into writing these observations,
which I'm sure many others will have made."

2. DISEMBODYING THE CAUSE

1. Indeed, Theseus's speech is so famous that it has been yoked in the service of
several arguments—pro- and anti-Art, pro- and anti-patriarchy—all of which insist on
its centrality to the play. But there has also been a strand of criticism, beginning with
René Girard ("Myth and Ritual in Shakespeare: *A Midsummer Night's Dream,*" in *Textual Strategies: Perspectives in Post-Structuralist Criticism,* ed. Josué V. Harari [Ithaca:
Cornell University Press, 1979], 189–212), which insists that Theseus's speech is less
important than Hippolyta's. For Girard, Hippolyta returns us to the idea of myth and
violence that he sees as central to the play's many doublings, suggesting that what we
find in Hippolyta's lines is an instance of "Shakespeare [being] more interested in [a]
systematically self-defeating type of passion than in the initial theme of 'true love'"
(189). For a reading that challenges the wisdom of Hippolyta as dramatic theorist, see
"Tragical Mirth: Framing Shakespeare's Hippolyta," in Kathryn Schwarz, *Tough Love:
Amazon Encounters in the English Renaissance* (Durham: Duke University Press, 2000),
203–35. In *Framing "India": The Colonial Imaginary in Early Modern Culture* (Stanford:
Stanford University Press, 2002). Shankar Raman makes an argument for a similarity
between Oberon and Titania's attitude toward the changeling Indian boy as an exotic
commodity from the East.

2. Unless otherwise specified, references to Shakespeare's plays are from *The Norton Shakespeare,* ed. Stephen Greenblatt et al., 2nd ed. (New York: W. W. Norton, 2008).

3. Lee Edelman, *No Future: Queer Theory and the Death Drive* (Durham: Duke
University Press, 2004), 25.

4. Jacques Lacan's theory of the mirror stage suggests that an "armour" is placed
around the "body in bits and pieces" as the self begins to form itself. This is done in
order so that the body—and by extension, the self—may be considered a uniform
whole, despite evidence to the contrary. See his essay on "The Mirror Stage as Forma-
tive of the Function of the I," in *Écrits: A Selection,* trans. Alan Sheridan (New York:
W. W. Norton, 1982), 1–6.

5. The changeling boy is, in Shankar Raman's words, "conspicuous only as an
absent center" (242). See his chapter "Indian Boys and Buskin'd Amazons: The Oedi-
pal Exchanges of *A Midsummer Night's Dream,*" in *Framing "India,"* 239–79.

6. See Margo Hendricks, "'Obscured by Dreams': Race, Empire, and Shakespeare's
A Midsummer Night's Dream," *Shakespeare Quarterly* 47, no. 1 (Spring 1996): 37–60.

7. Alain Badiou, *Metapolitics,* trans. Jason Barker (New York: Verso, 2005).

8. Sara Ahmed notes in *Queer Phenomenology* that "we don't know, as yet, what
shape such a world might take, or what mixtures might be possible, when we no longer
reproduce the lines we follow" (156).

9. See http://fuhgetabotit.newsvine.com/_news/2010/02/03/3849926-calling-out
-the-blatant-bigotry-of-neocon-editor-fox-man-bill-im-afraid-of-gays-krystal-the-econ
omist. See also Richard M. Ryan and William S. Ryan, "Homophobic? Maybe You're
Gay," *New York Times*, April 29, 2012, http://www.nytimes.com/2012/04/29/opinion
/sunday/homophobic-maybe-youre-gay.html?_r=1.

10. According to Shankar Raman, he exists "both as cause and resolution of the
play's dramatic action" (242). Jean-François Lyotard quotes André Green as saying (in
relation to theater in general and, for Lyotard, *Hamlet* in particular) that "the theatre
takes up the wager of invoking this absence in the most scandalous manner, since
nowhere does language hold forth with more ostentation the discourse of presence."
See "Jewish Oedipus," *Genre: Forms of Discourse and Culture* 10, no. 3 (Fall 1977):
395–411, 398. He goes on to add, again in relation to *Hamlet*, that "the complex function of representation in Shakespearean tragedy must be tied to the dimension of non-
fulfillment" (406).

11. Gary Jay Williams, *Our Moonlight Revels: "A Midsummer Night's Dream" in the
Theatre* (Iowa City: University of Iowa Press, 1997), 38. According to Trevor D.
Griffiths in *Shakespeare in Production: A Midsummer Night's Dream* (Cambridge: Cambridge University Press, 1996), "[T]here are only two known productions of the play
under its own name between 1660 and the 1816 production by Frederic Reynolds" (1).

12. According to Shankar Raman, "[The Indian boy's] absence is nothing less than
the immense distance that separates Europe from India, a distance double figured as
death. His presence is nothing less than a bridging of that distance in the form of
Europe's consumption of Eastern wares: Titania will not 'part' with the boy because
she has made him part of her" (244).

13. Griffiths notes that, despite the excision of this passage, "the changeling child
(the Indian boy) was a fixture in nineteenth-century productions" of the play (126).

14. Badiou, *Metapolitics*, 28.

15. As Henry S. Turner has so cogently pointed out in *Shakespeare's Double Helix*,
Shakespeare Now (London: Continuum, 2008), this play seems to muddle the distinctions between subjects and objects in ways that resemble what science-studies
writers like Bruno Latour theorize as the agency of objects.

16. See the introduction to Jonathan Gil Harris, ed., *Indography: Writing the
"Indian" in Early Modern England* (New York: Palgrave Macmillan, 2012), 1–20, for a
thorough mapping of the ways in which "India" signified in the sixteenth and seventeenth centuries.

17. Quoted in James Siemon, "'Nay That's Not Next': *Othello* V.ii in Performance,
1760–1900," *Shakespeare Quarterly* 37, no. 1 (Spring 1986): 38–51.

18. Badiou, *Saint Paul*, 58; emphasis mine.

19. Ibid.

20. Ibid., 79. This essay's indebtedness to Badiou's radical rereading of Paul to
reread *Othello* does not amount to an attempt to map Paul, even a Badiousian Paul,

onto the play. Rather, I have attempted to tease out some of the queer implications of what Badiou says, via Paul, about desire. However, for an excellent Pauline reading of *Othello*, see Julia Reinhard Lupton, *Citizen Saints: Shakespeare and Political Theology* (Chicago: University of Chicago Press, 2014), esp. chap. 1, "Othello Circumcised."

The effects of the event can be seen most clearly in the relation between desire and ontology. Here is Badiou's account of Paul's thinking about desire, an account that takes into consideration life, death, sin, and law, all of which are fully at play in Shakespeare's *Othello*:

> Paul's fundamental thesis is that the law, and only the law, endows desire with an autonomy sufficient for the subject of this desire, from the perspective of that autonomy, to come to occupy the place of the dead.
>
> The law is what gives life to desire. But in so doing, it constrains the subject so that he wants to follow only the path of death.
>
> What is sin exactly? It is not desire as such, for if it were one would not understand its link to the law and death. *Sin is the life of desire as autonomy, as automatism*. The law is required in order to unleash the automatic life of desire, the automatism of repetition. For only the law *fixes* the object of desire, binding desire to it regardless of the subject's "will." It is this objectal automatism of desire, inconceivable without the law, that assigns the subject to the carnal path of death.
>
> Clearly, what is at issue here is nothing less than the problem of the unconscious (Paul calls it the involuntary, what I do not want, *ho ou thelō*). The life of desire fixed and unleashed by the law is that which, decentered from the subject, accomplishes it as unconscious automatism, with respect to which the involuntary subject is capable only of inventing death. (79)

Desire does not bestow subjectivity. Instead, it condemns the subject to a life of death in which desire can neither be fulfilled nor explained. The automatic action of desire, separate from ownership of the self, is what Paul calls *ho ou thelō*—I do not do what I want to do. We can, of course, hear Othello's very name in this Greek New Testament formulation—that which is separated from desire. Badiou's "objectal automatism of desire, inconceivable without the law" connects also to something like Althusser's automated subject, whose interpellation guarantees that they articulate ideological prescription as the consummation of their own desires: "'That's obvious! That's right! That's true!'"

21. Sylvan Barnet, "Coleridge on Shakespeare's Villains, *Shakespeare Quarterly* 7, no. 1 (Winter 1956): 19.

22. This is exactly the kind of "probable" knowledge that Joel Altman exfoliates in "'Preposterous Conclusions,'" the essay that then went on to become the locus of his book, *The Improbablity of Othello: Rhetorical Anthropology and Shakespearean Selfhood* (Chicago: Chicago University Press, 2010). Noting that "*[Othello]* is informed by an economy of desire that is, in the deepest sense, improbable" (134), Altman notes that

the characters in the play trade on knowledge that seems probable to one another even though it is not grounded in cause.

23. Badiou, *Saint Paul*, 46.

24. This lack of causal support looms large in Thomas Rymer's excoriating early review of *Othello* (*The Critical Works of Thomas Rymer*, ed. Curt Zimansky [New Haven: Yale University Press, 1956], 132–64), a play he disliked intensely for straining the limits of our credulity. In a complaint picked up later by T. S. Eliot in his critique of *Hamlet* ("Hamlet and His Problems," in *The Sacred Wood* [New York: Alfred A. Knopf, 1921]) as lacking an "objective correlative" sufficient to bear the weight of the play's emotion, Rymer suggests Othello is improbable because it doles out its punishments (Desdemona's murder) and rewards (Othello's elevation to captain of the Venetian fleet) on the flimsiest of circumstances. The loss of a handkerchief leads to a murder, he scoffs, and a black man is made a Venetian captain: how improbable! Rymer does not explicitly mention the problem of desire even as everything he writes (including the improbability of Desdemona's being attracted to Othello) points toward it. Part of his sarcastic dismissal of the play involves the outlining what he terms the "moral" of the text: "First, This may be a caution to all Maidens of Quality how, / without their Parents consent, they run away with Blackamoors. / Secondly, This may be a warning to all good Wives, that they look / well to their Linnen. / Thirdly, This may be a lesson to Husbands, that before their / Jealousie be Tragical, the proofs may be Mathematical."

Clearly these are ridiculous morals for a tragedy worth its salt, and that is Rymer's point. Nonetheless, his mock-morals are of interest to readers of the play because he draws not one but three of them: one racist (white women should not elope with black men), one sexist (women should look after their household linen more carefully), and the third scientific (men should have mathematical proof—might we say cause?—before murdering their wives). Not one moral but three. Despite not explicitly using the word "cause," then, Rymer too cannot seem to pin down the meaning of the play; even his dismissal of the play comes up with too many reasons why. It is almost as though the moral of the tale cannot get over Desdemona's transgression against parental will in the first instance and simply rambles on after that. Because surely if you do not act on your desire and run away against your parents' wishes— Moral 1—then you need not have too much care of your linen closet since there will be no grounds for suspicion—Moral 2—which means the husband will not need to have mathematical proof because he will not be in the business of murdering his wife, thus making short shrift of Moral 3. Despite his satiric tone, then, Rymer intends the play to have only one moral: do not cross any boundaries in your desire and all will be well in the world. In addition, he asks potentially cuckolded husbands to get their facts straight before murdering their unfaithful wives; indeed, he asks them to get mathematical proof, since cause needs to be established clearly especially when it comes to desire and particularly when there might be none in sight.

The desire for desire not to cross boundaries cannot be realized, however, since the only identifying mark of desire is that it crosses boundaries: this is why laws and loves alike scramble to try and contain it. For Rymer, this transgressive desire is the root cause of all evil, particularly because it cannot be explained by cause. Why would a white woman run away with a Blackamoor anyway? Such causeless desire is also universal, by which I mean not only that everyone experiences it as such—which may or may not be true—but rather that everyone suffers its effects without knowing for sure its causes. This is why what one thinks of as one's own desire is in fact not owned by anyone. Desire both does and does not belong to a "one" that can be defined on the basis of that desire. This is probably why Othello says later on in his speech about cause: "Yet I'll not shed her blood, / Nor scar that whiter skin of hers than snow, / And smooth as monumental alabaster. / Yet she must die, else she'll betray more men" (5.2.1–6).

25. Othello smothers Desdemona, not wanting her to be penetrated in death. In *Season of Migration to the North*, Mustafa stabs Jean Morris, and there is blood everywhere.

26. Curiously, Brabantio is one of the few characters in the play who eventually grasps this causeless aspect of desire, although his knowledge does not help him cope any better with his daughter's preposterous desires. Initially, when faced with the reality of the Othello-Desdemona marriage, he states perplexedly: "For nature so prepost'rously to err— /Being not deficient, blind, or lame of sense— / Sans witchcraft could not" (1.3.75–77).

Desire must be understood; it needs to flow in orderly channels; otherwise the world as we know it will be at an end. Because we tend to follow in the footsteps of Brabantio's logic, the audience too can be counted on to reject the causelessness of desire and pick a cause for Desdemona's yearning for, and then murder by, Othello. But his daughter's marriage to Othello is an indicator late in Brabantio's life that desire cannot be kept in check, especially by the patriarchal law. This is why the father, after being overruled in his objection to the daughter's marriage, says spitefully to Othello: "Look to her, Moor, if thou hast eyes to see. / She has deceived her father, and may thee" (333–34). In an early echo of what Othello will bring up later in his "cause" speech, Brabantio talks about deceptions both near and far, of himself and of someone else, personal and universal.

27. If *Othello* stages such a Badiousian encounter with desire in which desire drains the self of ontology, then can we think of Othello *as* Badiou's Paul? After all, from the title of the play onward, Othello is presented as "The Moor of Venice," as a North African character in Venice whose self does not compute in any straightforward manner. Like Badiou's Paul, Shakespeare's Othello too finds himself, at a pivotal moment in his life, on the road to Damascus. As though allegorizing the Pauline event, Othello narrates a story about what happened on that road: "[I]n Aleppo once, / Where a malignant and a turbaned Turk / Beat a Venetian and traduced the state, / I took by th' throat the circumciséd dog / And smote him thus" (5.2.361–65). As the stage direction immediately following—*He stabs himself*—makes clear, Othello is here speaking about the divisions in himself that fail to render him as a coherent and unified subject.

Thus far, he echoes Paul's insistence on an evental division that militates against an ontological basis for the self. However, perhaps one of the reasons why *Othello* is a tragedy is that this anti-ontological thrust—so marked in Othello and Desdemona's mutual seduction that depends on traversing boundaries in tales of travel—is forgotten by the bearer of the news himself. Unlike Paul, who uses the event as the ground on which to encounter communities drained of their previous ontological tags—the Jews are no longer known by their law, the Greeks by their philosophy—Othello appears to hold on to the ontological markers for both Venetian and Turk. Othello's combination of two ontologies extends an identitarian additive framework that is unlike Paul's subtractive one. Not fully enjoying the uncoupling of desire from ontology brings only death to the play's hero. At the very least, Othello's fate should serve as a warning to the ontologists among us.

3. Lesbians without Borders

1. See Musharraf Ali Farooqi, trans., *The Adventures of Amir Hamza* (New York: Random House, 2007), for more details of this iconic *dastan*.

2. I am greatly indebted to Mahmood Farooqui's blogspot—http://dastangoi.blog spot.in/2010/02/what-is-dastangoi.html—for these details about the history of *dastangoi*.

3. For the Sufis, if the poetry of the *ghazal* derived from Persian, then it was easy to maintain the indeterminate character of the beloved since Persian is a genderless language; if the poetry was in Urdu, then the beloved was gendered male because the love of women was not considered exalted enough to be the subject of mystical music. Either way, the Sufis performed male homoerotic desire despite or because of its metaphysical convolutions.

4. *Dastan* literature belongs to a long and rich line of texts that Mohamad Tavakoli-Targi in *Refashioning Iran: Orientalism, Occidentalism and Historiography* (New York: Palgrave, 2001) terms "homeless texts," by which he refers to the "large corpus of texts made homeless with the emergence of *history with borders*, a convention that confined historical writing to the borders of modern nation-states" (9).

5. Frances W. Pritchett, *Nets of Awareness: Urdu Poetry and Its Critics* (New Delhi: Katha, 2004), 140. This passage is a quotation from the *Water of Life* by Urdu poet and literary critic Muhammad Husain Azad.

6. See Tariq Rahman's excellent study, *From Hindi to Urdu: A Social and Political History* (New Delhi: Orient Blackswan, 2011), for an account of the trajectory by which Urdu came to be called Urdu. The name "Urdu" was first used only around 1780, and then the ideological/religious/identitarian baggage was subsequently layered onto it in the decades that followed.

7. English is seen as being completely separate from French; historically, this difference in language has served as the distinguishing feature between the hardy English and the effete French; see, for instance, Shakespeare's history play *Henry V* about the glories of England and English in opposition to the French.

8. Pritchett elaborates on this double movement: (1) the identification of Urdu poetry with a "play of words," and (2) a Victorian disdain for that play when compared to the instrumentality of the English language: "Plainness and directness, this disdain for literary niceties, this concern with the real world, is part of what Azad wants from English. . . . English shows us how to use language instrumentally, how to short-circuit the play of words, how to get from feelings in the poet's heart to feelings in the reader's heart with a minimum of fuss in between. Mere words may be suspect, the autonomous 'game of words' may have been discredited—but feelings are reassuringly real and irreproachably 'natural'" (143).

9. Ruth Vanita and Saleem Kidwai, eds., *Same-Sex Love in India: A Literary History* (New Delhi: Penguin, 2008), 250.

10. Pritchett, *Nets of Awareness*, 167.

11. Vanita and Kidwai, *Same-Sex Love in India*, 220.

12. Ibid., 251.

13. Salim Kidwai puts this last point in another way: "The [post–nineteenth-century] denigration of *iham goi* [self-conscious poetry with multiple meanings] as serious poetry coincides with the time when homoeroticism in Urdu poetry begins to disappear" (140).

14. This is Pritchett's rendition of Sadiq's argument; many of the phrases are hers, some are Sadiq's; see Pritchett, *Nets of Awareness*, xiv.

15. For more details about the nineteenth century's critical response to Shakespeare's Sonnets, see Margreta de Grazia, "The Scandal of Shakespeare's Sonnets," in *Shakespeare Survey*, vol. 46, *Shakespeare and Sexuality,* ed. Stanley Wells (Cambridge: Cambridge University Press, 1993, Cambridge Collections Online, May 30, 2012, DOI:10.1017/CCOL0521450276.004).

16. http://dastangoi.blogspot.in/2010/02/what-is-dastangoi.html.

17. Alain Badiou, "Rhapsody for the Theatre: A Short Philosophical Treatise," trans. Bruno Bosteels, *Theatre Survey* 49, no. 2 (November 2008): 187–238.

18. See M. M. Bakhtin, "The Epic and the Novel: Towards a Methodology for the Study in the Novel," in *The Dialogic Imagination*, ed. Michael Holquist (Austin: University of Texas Press, 1981), 3–40.

19. See the OED entry for "rhapsody," definitions 2a and 4.

20. For an interdisciplinary analysis of our compulsion to "situate" ourselves in reference to specific locations and identities while ignoring the politics of universality, see David Simpson, *Situatedness; or, Why we Keep Saying Where We're Coming From* (Durham: Duke University Press, 2002).

21. This, and all other translations from Hindi and Urdu, are my own.

22. For a theorization of the theater that has a similar impetus, see Gilles Deleuze, *Difference and Repetition*, trans. Paul Patton (London: Continuum, 2004), where he argues for "a new theatre or a new (non-Aristotelian) interpretation of the theatre; a theatre of multiplicities opposed in every respect to the theatre of representation, which leaves intact neither the identity of the thing represented, nor author, nor spectator,

nor character, nor representation which, through vicissitudes of the play, can become the object of a production of knowledge or final recognition" (241). For an idea of a subtractive theater, see also Deleuze, "One Less Manifesto," in *Mimesis, Masochism, and Mime*, ed. Timothy Murray (Ann Arbor: University of Michigan Press, 1997), 239–58.

23. Vijaydan Detha, *Chouboli and Other Stories*, vol. 1, trans. Christi A. Merrill, with Kailash Kabir (New York: Fordham University Press [in association with Katha]. 2011).

24. See my chapter on plagiarism and desire in *Unhistorical Shakespeare: Queer Theory in Shakespearean Literature and Film* (New York: Palgrave, 2008), 73–94.

25. See Jacques Lacan, *The Four Fundamental Concepts of Psychoanalysis: The Seminar of Jacques Lacan, Book XI*, trans. Alan Sheridan (New York: W. W. Norton, 1998).

26. All references to "Shahzadi Chouboli Boli" are from Mahmmod Farooqui and Danish Husain's unpublished working manuscript.

27. http://www.indiana.edu/~jofr/review.php?id=1254.

28. This claim was introduced in the second performance that I saw. As with Greek rhapsodies, *dastans* too change their tune for each singing, and their face for each showing.

29. C. M. Naim, "Transvestic Words? The Rekhti in Urdu," *The Annual of Urdu Studies* 16 (2001): part 1, 3–26.

30. Its reputed creator was one Sa'adat Yar Khan "Rangin" (died 1834–35), a famous poet associated with Lucknow. Other authors include Insha' Allah Khan "Insha" (died 1817), Qalandar Bakhsh "Jur'at" (died 1810), and Mir Yar Ali Khan "Jan Sahib" (1818–97).

31. Naim, "Transvestic Words?," 17.

32. Ruth Vanita, "'Married among Their Companions': Female Homoerotic Relations in Nineteenth-Century Urdu *Rekhti* Poetry," in *Journal of Women's History* 16, no. 1 (2004): 12–53.

33. Ibid.

34. This refusal to see unconventional possibilities is also a mode of indifference, but it is one that merely reaffirms its own ontological assumptions. This is not indifference in the Badiousian, evental, sense, which necessitates an anti-ontology that calls into question all the identities one thought one owned.

35. Sigmund Freud, *New Introductory Lectures on Psycho-Analysis*, in *Complete Psychological Works of Sigmund Freud*, ed. James Strachey (New York: W. W. Norton, 1990), 100.

CODA

1. The historian Ayesha Jalal asks the question in this way in *The Pity of Partition: Manto's Life, Times, and Work across the India-Pakistan Divide* (Noida: HarperCollins, 2013): "[How can] the contours of the cultural nation, creatively and broadly construed [be made to] map neatly onto the limited boundaries of the political nation?" (12).

2. Germany is a notable exception precisely because religion was not invoked as the basis on which to institute difference. In fact, German partition was not based on ontologizing particularity at all—it was based on a jockeying for geopolitical power that collapsed when the ideological distinctions on which it was premised themselves collapsed.

3. Lauren Berlant and Lee Edelman, *Sex, or the Unbearable* (Durham: Duke University Press, 2013).

4. See my *Unhistorical Shakespeare*.

5. Alain Badiou, *Being and Event*, trans. Oliver Feltham (London: Continuum, 2007).

Index

MADHAVI MENON is professor of English at Ashoka University. She is the author of *Wanton Words: Rhetoric and Sexuality in English Renaissance Drama, Unhistorical Shakespeare: Queer Theory in Shakespearean Literature and Film,* and editor of *Shakesqueer: A Queer Companion to the Complete Works of Shakespeare.*